MOLECULAR DYNAMICS

Edited by **Alexander Vakhrushev**

Molecular Dynamics
http://dx.doi.org/10.5772/intechopen.70978
Edited by Alexander Vakhrushev

Contributors

Alberto Pais, Tânia Firmino Cova, Sandra Nunes, Bruce Milne, Andreia Jorge, Monica Pickholz, Juan Albano, Eneida De Paula, Sergiy Kotrechko, Nataliya Stetsenko, Igor Mikhailovskij, Ovsjannikov Oleksandr, Aylin Ahadi, Per Hansson, Solveig Melin, Alexander Vasilevich Vakhrushev

Notice

Statements and opinions expressed in the chapters are these of the individual contributors and not necessarily those of the editors or publisher. No responsibility is accepted for the accuracy of information contained in the published chapters. The publisher assumes no responsibility for any damage or injury to persons or property arising out of the use of any materials, instructions, methods or ideas contained in the book.

First published in London, United Kingdom, 2018 by IntechOpen
IntechOpen is the global imprint of INTECHOPEN LIMITED, registered in England and Wales, registration number: 11086078, The Shard, 25th floor, 32 London Bridge Street
London, SE19SG – United Kingdom
Printed in Croatia

British Library Cataloguing-in-Publication Data
A catalogue record for this book is available from the British Library

Additional hard copies can be obtained from orders@intechopen.com

Molecular Dynamics, Edited by Alexander Vakhrushev
p. cm.
Print ISBN 978-1-78923-524-1
Online ISBN 978-1-78923-525-8

We are IntechOpen,
the world's leading publisher of
Open Access books
Built by scientists, for scientists

3,650+
Open access books available

114,000+
International authors and editors

118M+
Downloads

151
Countries delivered to

Our authors are among the

Top 1%
most cited scientists

12.2%
Contributors from top 500 universities

Interested in publishing with us?
Contact book.department@intechopen.com

Numbers displayed above are based on latest data collected.
For more information visit www.intechopen.com

Meet the editor

Vakhrushev Alexander Vasilyevich received his PhD degree in Technical Sciences from the Izhevsk Institute of Mechanical Engineering, Russia, in 1982 and his Doctor of Sciences degree in Physics and Mathematics from the Institute of Continuous Media Mechanics, Ural Branch of the Russian Academy of Sciences, Russia, in 2003. Currently, he is the Head of the Department of Nanotechnology and Microsystems, Kalashnikov Izhevsk State Technical University and the Head of the Department of Mechanics of Nanostructures, Institute of Mechanics, Udmurt Federal Research Center, Ural Branch of the Russian Academy of Sciences. He has published over 400 publications. His research interests include multiscale mathematical modeling of physical-chemical processes into the nanohetero systems.

Contents

Preface

This book is devoted to a description of the modeling of nanosystems and a detailed exposition of the application of molecular dynamics methods to problems from various fields of technology: material science, the formation of composite molecular complexes, and transport of nanosystems. The research results of the modeling of various nanosystems are presented: soft supramolecular nanostructures, metallic nanosized crystals, nanosized beams of single-crystal Cu, and drug delivery systems.

A collection of five scientific chapters on the application of molecular dynamics methods to the simulation of different nanosystems is presented. Each chapter represents a comprehensive study.

Chapter 1 is devoted to the analysis of the value of the method of molecular dynamics for solving the problem "Designing Materials with Controlled Properties" of the modern industrial revolution "Production 4.0."

Chapter 2 presents the theoretical background of the molecular dynamics simulations of the design and assembly of soft supramolecular structures based on small building blocks and also provides an overview of the available MD-based methods, including path-based and alchemical-free energy calculations. Practical instructions on the selection of methods and post-treatment procedures are introduced. Relevant examples in which noncovalent interactions dominate are presented. Several examples are presented in which simulations are used for establishing the contributions of NCI to the free energy in systems: host-guest complexes, polyelectrolytes, and proteins.

In **Chapter 3**, the atomic mechanisms governing the strength of nanosized metallic crystals on the basis of size and orientation effects, the temperature dependence of strength and atomism of fracture of body-centered cubic crystals under triaxial uniform (hydrostatic) tension, and the concept of local instability are described. The molecular dynamics simulations and experimental studies of the deformation and failure of tungsten and molybdenum nanocrystals are presented. Simulation methods based on the molecular dynamics methods and extended Finnis-Sinclair semi-empirical potential are used. The *in situ* mechanical loading of nanosized crystals in the field-induced mechanical experiments is realized using the Maxwell mechanical stress induced by high-electric fields.

Chapter 4 presents the molecular dynamics simulations of nanosized beams of single-crystal Cu with two different crystallographic orientations and with square-shaped defects, loaded in displacement-controlled tension until ruptured. Research methods are based on the molecular dynamics methods and used a program LAMMPS with an EAM potential for modeling the atomic interactions. Simulation showed various processes of plastic deformation in the field of defects and allowed to establish the complex behavior of defects.

Chapter 5 presents different applications of atomistic and coarse-grain (CG) molecular dynamics simulations to drug delivery systems (DDSs). An excellent detailed review of the modeling in this area is also presented. Different applications of drug delivery carriers, such as liposomes, polymeric micelles, and polymersomes using atomistic and CG molecular dynamics simulations, are investigated.

The information from this book will be useful for engineers, technologists, researchers, and postgraduate students interested in the study of the whole complex of computer simulation based on the concept of molecular dynamics methods for the task of designing and producing nanomaterials and nanosystems with controlled properties.

I would like to express my appreciation to all the contributors of this book. My special thanks go to the Author Service Manager, **Ms. Anita Condic**, and other staff at InTech publishing for their kind support and great efforts in bringing this book to completion.

Prof. Alexander Vakhrushev
Head of Department Mechanics of Nanostructures
Institute of Mechanics, Udmurt Federal Research Center
Ural Branch of the Russian Academy of Sciences, Russia

Head of Department Nanotechnology and Microsystems
Kalashnikov Izhevsk State Technical University, Russia

Introductory Chapter: Molecular Dynamics: Basic Tool of Nanotechnology Simulations for "Production 4.0" Revolution

Alexander V. Vakhrushev

Additional information is available at the end of the chapter

http://dx.doi.org/10.5772/intechopen.79045

1. Introduction

One of the main tasks of the modern industrial revolution "Production 4.0" is the translation of all processes preceding the actual receipt of a new product in a digital representation. Forecasts for the development of this stage of production point to the ever-increasing value of computer modeling, the urgency of which will constantly increase. It is expected that computer modeling will be invested more financial and intellectual resources. This is especially relevant for one of the main tasks of the industrial revolution "Production 4," called "designing materials with controlled properties," which is the basis for the development of effective biotechnologies and nanotechnologies. A full and exact solution to this complex problem is impossible without considering the properties and processes of the formation of materials with controlled properties at the atomic and nanoscale of mathematical description and modeling.

However, specific feature of the physical processes in nanoscale systems is that the key phenomena determining the behavior of a nanoscale system in real time at the macroscale take place at small space and time scales [1, 2]. Many experimental and theoretical studies have shown that the properties of a nanoscale system depend not only on the properties of its constituent elements but also on the regularities of the spatial arrangement of the nanoelements in nanosystem and the parameters of the nanoelements interaction.

In this perspective, the molecular dynamics, which allows to describe the formation, evolution, and properties of the above-mentioned nanosystems in a sufficiently complete and precise manner, should become one of the methods for calculating and modeling modern engineers and technologists. This is explained by the fact that molecular dynamics, being a powerful tool of scientific research, is increasingly becoming a full-fledged stage in obtaining new materials, creating a new technological process and designing a new product at the nanoscale level. This process was observed in the 1960–1980s of the last century with respect to the finite element method and led to the fact that this method is now being applied well and confidently by modern engineers and technologists in the creation of new materials and machines. We can expect that the process of industrial revolution "Production 4.0" method of molecular dynamics will be adopted as an instrument of engineers and technologists.

However, this will only be the beginning of a deeper penetration of modeling into digital production. It should be noted that, at present, in modern scientific research methods of modeling, the molecular dynamics is usually the key element of a more complex and comprehensive multilevel mathematical modeling comprising multiple spatial and temporal scales [3–5]. The main stages of such a multi-level modeling of nanosystems are quantum modeling, molecular dynamics, mesomechanics and continuum mechanics.

The calculation of the configurations of a molecular formation, which are the constituents of a nanoparticle, is based on the quantum mechanics ("ab initio") methods of modeling. These methods give the most complete and precise presentation of nano-objects and take into account quantum effects, but they are very intensive computationally. At present, the use of the quantum mechanics methods for the calculation of nanoscale systems is limited to 1000–2000 atoms composing a nanoscale system.

The modeling of the coalescence of molecules into nanoelements can be performed by the molecular dynamics method. The method allows to consider systems containing up to 10 million atoms and more than that, but it does not take into account quantum phenomena.

The calculation of the movement of nanoelements and their coalescence is the task for mesodynamics. The characteristic feature of mesodynamics is the simultaneous use of the methods of molecular and classical dynamics.

It should also be noted that a number of phenomena, in particular, the phenomena taking place at the final stages of the nanoscale system formation, can be considered within the framework of continuum mechanics.

Each of the above methods has its own advantages and limitations. The use of any of the above methods of modeling or their combination for specific nanotechnology problems depends on the calculation accuracy required.

One can point to a number of problems of such modeling listed below:

- multiscale nature and connectedness of problems,
- large number of variables,
- variation of scales both over space and in time,
- characteristic times of processes at different scales differ by orders of magnitude,
- variation of the problem variables at different scales of modeling,

- matching of boundary conditions at the transition from one modeling scale to another when the problem variables are changed,

- stochastic behavior of nanoscale systems.

Molecular dynamics allows us to proceed correctly from the study of atomic and molecular processes by methods of quantum mechanics to the study of processes at the macrolevel by the methods of continuous medium mechanics. The main problem here is the matching of the boundary conditions of the modeling problems at each space-time scale.

Thus, we can distinguish two main functions of molecular dynamics:

- the method of modeling the processes of nanosystem formation and theoretical analysis of their properties

- the bridge connecting the various stages of multilevel modeling of nanosystems.

Based on the foregoing, the purpose of this book is to describe a number of problems in the modeling of nanosystems and a detailed exposition of the application of molecular dynamics methods to problems from various fields of technology: material science, the formation of composite molecular complexes, transport of nanosystems, etc. The book summarizes the research results of the authors in the field of modeling of various nanosystems: soft supramolecular nanostructures, nano-sized beams of single-crystal Cu, metallic nanosized crystals, drug delivery systems, and systems stabilized by hydrogen bonds.

The study of the materials of this book can be the beginning of the reader's study of the whole complex of modeling based on the concept of molecular dynamics modeling.

In addition, it should be noted that the research materials dynamics methods presented in the book can be the basis for the development of artificial intelligence methods in relation to the problem "designing materials with controlled properties."

To get more complete information about the methods of molecular dynamics and its significance in the overall complex multilevel task of modeling nanosystems and nanomaterials, the novice reader can get additional information from the list of literature. In this list of papers and books, the works [6–23] to modeling by methods of quantum mechanics, works [24–31] to molecular dynamics, and works [32, 33] to mesodynamics are devoted.

Author details

Alexander V. Vakhrushev[1,2]*

*Address all correspondence to: vakhrushev-a@yandex.ru

1 Department of Mechanics of Nanostructure, Institute of Mechanics, Udmurt Federal Research Center, Ural Branch of the Russian Academy of Science, Izhevsk, Russia

2 Department of Nanotechnology and Microsystems, Kalashnikov Izhevsk State Technical University, Izhevsk, Russia

References

[1] Drexler E, Peterson C, Pergamit G. Unbounding the Future: The Nanotechnology Revolution. New York: William M. and Company, Inc; 1991. 158p

[2] Imry Y. Introduction to Mesoscopic Physics. Oxford: University Press; 2002. 304p

[3] Martin Steinhauser O. Computational Multiscale Modelling of Fluids and Solids. Theory and Application. Berlin–Heidelberg: Springer-Verlag; 2008. 427p

[4] Weinan E. Principles of Multiscale Modeling. Cambridge: Cambridge University Press; 2011. 466p

[5] Vakhrushev AV. Computational Multiscale Modeling of Multiphase Nanosystems. Theory and Applications. Waretown, New Jersey, USA: Apple Academic Press; 2017. 402p

[6] Bader RFW. Atoms in Molecules. A Quantum Theory. Oxford: Clarendon Press; 1990. 434p

[7] Bischof C, Bucker M. Computing derivatives of computer programs. In: Grotendorst J, editor. Modern Methods and Algorithms of Quantum Chemistry. Vol. 1. Julich: John von Neumann Institute for Computing; 2000. pp. 287-299. NIC Series

[8] Brooks BR, Bruccoleri RE, Olafson BD, States DJ, Swaminathan S, Karplus M. CHARMM: A program for macromolecular energy minimization, and dynamics calculations. Journal of Computational Chemistry. 1983;2:187-217

[9] Cagın T, Che J, Qi Y, Zhou Y, Demiralp E, Gao G, Goddard W III. Computational materials chemistry at the nanoscale. Journal of Nanoparticle Research. 1999;1:51-69

[10] Frenkel D, Smit B. Understanding Molecular Simulation: From Algorithms to Applications. New York: Academic Press; 2002. 638p

[11] Frisch MJ, Trucks GW, Schlegel HB, Scuseria GE, Robb MA, Cheeseman JR, et al. Gaussian 98 (Revision A.1). Pittsburgh, PA: Gaussian Inc; 1998

[12] Gauss J. Molecular properties. In: Grotendorst J, editor. Modern methods and algorithms of quantum chemistry, proceedings. 2nd ed. Vol. 3. Julich: John von Neumann Institute for Computing; 2000. pp. 541-592. NIC Series

[13] Gramer CJ. Essentials of Computational Chemistry. Theories and Models. Second ed. New Jersey: Wiley; 2009. 596p

[14] Lipkowitz KB, Boyd DB, editors. Reviews in Computational Chemistry. Vol. 16. New York: Wiley-VCH; 2000. 210p

[15] Lindahl E, Hess B, van der Spoel D. Gromacs 3.0: A package for molecular simulation and trajectory analysis. Journal of Molecular Modeling. 2001;7:306-317

[16] Marx D, Hutter J. Ab Initio Molecular Dynamics: Theory and Advanced Methods. New York: Cambridge University Press; 2009. 567p

[17] MacKerell AD Jr, Banavali N, Foloppe N. Development and current status of the CHARMM force field for nucleic acids. Biopolymers. 2001;**56**:257-265

[18] Mercle CR. Computational nanotechnology. Nanotechnology. 1991;**2**:134-141

[19] Merkle CR. It's a small, small, small, small world. MIT Technology Review. 1997;**100**:25-32

[20] Parr RG, Yang W. Density-Functional Theory of Atoms and Molecules. Oxford: Oxford University Press; 1989. 331pp

[21] Ramachandran KI, Deepa G, Namboori K. Computational Chemistry and Molecular Modelling. Berlin Heidelberg: Springer-Verlag; 2010. 397p

[22] Sholl DS, Stecker JA. Density Functional Theory. A Practical Introduction. New Jersey: Wiley; 2009. 328p

[23] McWeeny R. Methods of Molecular Quantum Mechanics. Second ed. London: Academic Press; 1996. 591p

[24] Anderson HS. Molecular dynamics simulation at constant pressure and/or temperature. The Journal of Chemical Physics. 1980;**72**:2384-2396

[25] Allen MP, Tildesley DJ. Computer Simulation of Liquids. New York, Oxford: Science Publications; 1987. 400p

[26] Burkert U, Allinger NL. Molecular Mechanics. Washington, D.C.: American Chemical Society; 1982

[27] Haile MJ. Molecular Dynamics Simulation–Elementary Methods. New York: Wiley Interscience; 1992. 386p

[28] Heerman WD. Computer Simulation Methods in Theoretical Physics. Berlin: Springer-Verlag; 1986. 145p

[29] Leach AR. Molecular Modelling. Principles and Applications. Edinburgh: Pearson Education Limited; 2001. 773p

[30] Phillips JC et al. Scalable molecular dynamics with NAMD. Computational Chemistry. 2005;**26**:1781-1802

[31] Plimpton SJ. Fast parallel algorithms for short-range molecular dynamics. Journal of Computational Physics. 1995;**117**:1-19

[32] Holian BL. Formulating mesodynamics for polycrystalline materials. Europhysics Letters. 2003;**64**:330-336

[33] Vakhrouchev AV. Simulation of nano-elements interactions and self-assembling. Modelling and Simulation in Materials Science and Engineering. 2006;**14**:975-991

Chapter 2

Modeling Soft Supramolecular Nanostructures by Molecular Simulations

Tânia F. Cova, Sandra C. Nunes, Bruce F. Milne,
Andreia F. Jorge and Alberto C. Pais

Additional information is available at the end of the chapter

http://dx.doi.org/10.5772/intechopen.74939

Abstract

The design and assembly of soft supramolecular structures based on small building blocks are governed by non-covalent interactions, selective host-guest interactions, or a combination of different interaction types. There is a surprising number of studies supporting the use of computational models for mimicking supramolecular nanosystems and studying the underlying patterns of molecular recognition and binding, in multi-dimensional approaches. Based on physical properties and mathematical concepts, these models are able to provide rationales for the conformation, solvation and thermodynamic characterization of this type of systems. Molecular dynamics (MD), including free-energy calculations, yield a direct coupling between experimental and computational investigation. This chapter provides an overview of the available MD-based methods, including path-based and alchemical free-energy calculations. The theoretical background is briefly reviewed and practical instructions are introduced on the selection of methods and post-treatment procedures. Relevant examples in which non-covalent interactions dominate are presented.

Keywords: molecular dynamics, free-energy, non-covalent interactions, host-guest systems, supramolecular structures

1. Introduction

In the past 3 decades, atomistic simulations and free-energy calculations have emerged as indispensable tools to tackle deep chemical and biological questions that experiment has left unresolved. To fully understand the vast majority of chemical and biological processes, it is often necessary to examine their underlying free-energy behavior [1]. This is the case, for instance, of phase diagrams, protein-ligand and drug binding affinities, drug partitioning, reaction rates, equilibrium constants, acid-base equilibria, solvation contributions, or confinement energies. The prediction of these quantities, with relevance in the field of computer-aided drug design requires knowledge of the related free-energy changes [2]. Most of the research topics involving molecular modeling and simulation, with free-energy calculations, stem from pharmaceutical applications [1, 3, 4]. Those methods have provided insight into the time evolution of host-guest systems and of protein-ligand interactions [2, 4] and have revealed the respective dynamic behavior in water, thus establishing relevant recognition and affinity patterns. However, the formation of inclusion complexes is frequently used as a drug solubilizing approach, aiming at better therapeutic outcomes. This makes results sparse and focused on individual systems, lacking a comprehensive characterization for assessing the factors that govern, for example, the inclusion process. Despite the continuous progress and development of improved algorithms, the estimation of binding free energies by molecular dynamics (MD) simulations still requires significant computational efforts due to the mathematical complexity imposed by the solvated systems, often composed by myriads of atoms [3]. Recently, Pais and co-workers [5] have proposed an automated procedure based on umbrella sampling and the "flexible molecule" approximation for the calculation of binding constants in complexes formed between β-cyclodextrin and several naphthalene derivatives. In this type of complexes, the guest molecule may alter the structure of the host, leading to relevant cooperative effects, when compared to the free molecules. Inclusion of guests into host molecules is essentially governed by (i) relatively weak non-covalent interactions (NCI), including hydrophobic, van der Waals and electrostatic interactions, π-π stacking, hydrogen bonding, or a combination of these interactions, and also by (ii) stronger ionic and dipolar interactions. In addition to several reviews (see e.g. [6, 7]), including many dealing with specific host-guest systems [4, 7–12], a large number of research papers are available on this subject, including some focused on mechanistic aspects of the inclusion phenomena (see e.g. Refs. [5, 13–15].)

In fact, both the efficiency and accuracy of free-energy calculations have been greatly improved by a wide variety of methods [16]. However, it is increasingly difficult for researchers to find their way through the maze of available computational techniques. Why are there so many methods? Are they conceptually related? Do they differ in efficiency and accuracy? Why do methods that appear to be very similar carry different names? Which method is the best for a specific problem? How to choose the most relevant method to tackle the system at hand? These questions may leave researchers in the field confused and looking for clear guidelines. However, answers to these questions are not straightforward. A distinction has been made between two classes of free-energy transformations, namely those of alchemical and geometrical nature [17]. While the former exploits the malleability of the potential energy function and the virtually infinite possibilities of computer simulations to transform between chemically distinct states, the latter includes positional, orientational, and conformational changes in macromolecules and complexes thereof. At the practical level, such transformations are achieved using a variety of approaches, which can be separated into four main groups, (i) probability distributions and histograms, (ii) perturbation theory, (iii) non-equilibrium work and (iv) gradient-based methods [18]. One recurrent question concerns the selection of the most relevant approach to tackle the problem at hand, which can be reworded in terms of the best-suited, cost-effective method to obtain a reliable answer. To a large extent, this question can be addressed by considering the actual nature of the transformation, alchemical, or geo-metrical, and subsequently by deciding which one, among the aforementioned methods, is more likely to yield the desired free-energy change at a minimal computational effort.

A detailed overview of the concepts and fundamentals of the available methods for estimating free energies is given in Ref. [16]. The guiding principle is that most of these are based on a few fundamental assumptions, devised by some pioneers in the field [19–23]. With some exceptions, more recent contributions are not based on innovative fundamental principles, but are "astute and ingenious ways of applying those already known" [16].

2. Context and relevant aspects

In the context of non-covalent binding, host-guest systems have emerged as useful models for assessing the accuracy of simulation methods. This can be explained by the fact that these systems display interesting features comparable to protein-ligand binding, including hydrogen bonds, conformational restriction and desolvation, and also possess an adequate size for conducting more precise thermodynamic calculations [24]. This is the case of cyclodextrin host-guest systems, which mimic several characteristics of protein-ligand binding with the advantage of being much more accessible due to their small size. These characteristics also facilitate the selection of the force field (FF) based on the attribution of the level of accuracy.

Specifically, the combination of MD and free-energy calculations with experimental results have revealed the relevant interaction patterns in the formation of inclusion complexes between several host (e.g. cyclodextrins [4, 5], cucurbiturils [25] and bambusurils [8, 26]) and guest molecules (e.g. antitumor and antiviral drugs [27], steroids [28], flavonoids [29] and small ionic species [26]). These small aggregates, comprising typically two (in 1:1 host-guest complexes) or three molecules (in 1:2 complexes) have been the basis of fundamental developments for establishing what governs associations in soft-matter and stability in larger supramolecular nanostructures, such as nanogels and targeted nanoparticles.

Despite significant advances in molecular modeling techniques and the comparative simplicity of host-guest systems, there is still a need for a tractable and theoretically sound computational method to interpret experimental data and help with the design of new hosts for targeted molecular guests. Similarly to other macromolecular systems, host-guest systems exhibit marked entropy-enthalpy compensation. Such property has been observed for NCI in both water and organic solvents. Among the wide applications of alchemical transformations, host-guest chemistry occupies the most prominent position [30].

A fundamental aspect to be understood is the precise manner in which the guest molecule binds to the host. MD simulations have greatly contributed to understanding molecular binding phenomena as a fully dynamical process. However, these simulations are limited by the time scales that can be routinely sampled. The introduction of special-purpose machines and the evolution of parallel codes, has increased enormously the time scales accessible by fully atomistic MD. However, guest molecules (e.g. drugs) with long residence times are common, and the respective association/dissociation from a host or receptor cannot be observed by conventional MD calculations even when specialized hardware is employed. This well-recognized limitation of MD has led to the development of various algorithms to enhance the sampling of the high free-energy states and rare events, associated to high free-energy barriers.

Enhanced sampling methods can speed up conformational sampling by various means and represent an effective alternative to access with high accuracy the thermodynamics and possibly the kinetics that underlie these processes. Steered MD and umbrella sampling [31], with potential of mean force estimation (PMF) [32] allows inspecting the free-energy profile and the mechanistic aspects involved in formation of host-guest complexes [5].

In recent years, other strategies aimed at the same goal have been proposed. Replica exchange [33] metadynamics [34, 35], accelerated MD [36], milestoning [37], transition path sampling [38], and combinations of these are among the most widely used methods to enhance conformational sampling. For instance, the replica exchange methodology has been used in the atomistic simulations, as well as in a number of coarse-grained simulations (see e.g. [34]). This method has been applied to study free-energy landscape and folding mechanisms of several peptides and proteins [33], through several variants of the traditional temperature dependent scheme, available in some of the most popular MD packages, such as AMBER [39], GROMACS [40] and NAMD [41].

Among the enhanced sampling methods that fully explore the binding mechanism, metadynamics, especially in the well-tempered formulation, has emerged as a powerful approach for accelerating rare events [35]. This has been applied in drug docking to protein and enzymes, systems involving big conformational changes and relevant solvation effects. Directed dynamics such as the adaptive biasing force (ABF) and hyperdynamics were also derived from the same principles as adopted by metadynamics [35]. The implementation of metadynamics in MD codes, such as NAMD and GROMACS, have promoted a broad range of applications of the method, ranging from solid state physics to biological systems.

The adaptive biasing force algorithm (ABF) has also emerged as a promising strategy for mapping complex free-energy landscapes [42, 43], as it combines both constrained and unconstrained simulations into a highly efficient scheme, providing an uniform sampling of the order parameter. Briefly, as a simulation progresses, a continuously updated biasing force is added to the equations of motion, such that in the long-time limit it produces a Hamiltonian devoid of an average force acting along the transition coordinate of interest. In contrast to umbrella sampling schemes, based on probability distribution functions, ABF uses forces, which can be readily estimated without the need to sample broad ranges of the order parameter.

Another relevant problem in the early estimations of free-energy is related to the strong dependence on system size, in the presence of significant electrostatic interactions [44]. Once long-range corrections using Ewald lattice summation or the reaction field are included in molecular simulations, size effects in neutral systems decrease markedly. The problem, however, persists in charged systems, for example in determining the free energy of charging a neutral species in solution. In this context, it has been demonstrated that system-size dependence can be largely eliminated in these cases by careful treatment of the self-interaction term, which is associated with interactions of charged particles with their periodic images and a uniform neutralizing charge background [44].

The ability to decouple relevant energy contributions from individual components is also far from a simple solution, being the basis of alchemical free-energy methods [19, 20], such as the thermodynamic integration (TI) [17, 44, 45], free-energy perturbation (FEP) [20] and molecular mechanics-Poisson-Boltzmann surface area (MM-PBSA) [46].

The feasibility of the estimated binding free-energy depends on the correct estimation of thermodynamic quantities and the concerted interaction components (enthalpy, entropy and solvent contributions) [15, 47]. For instance, the quantification of these interaction components have been directed at inclusion complexes between cyclodextrins and its derivatives and different model drugs (see Refs. [13, 15, 48].). However, only a few studies (e.g. [5, 13]) have introduced technical and practical directions to investigate the energy components underlying the stability of these complexes. Spoel and co-workers [13] have emphasized the role of solvent contribution resorting to steered molecular dynamics and PMF calculations. The latter techniques have also been used by Pais and co-workers [5] for assessing the relevance of non-included guest moieties in the binding constants of cyclodextrin inclusion complexes, estimating the weight of enthalpic and entropic contributions to the free-energy. In this context, MD and PMF calculations allow the modulation of the formation processes in inclusion complexes, along which the free-energy profiles are derived from an umbrella sampling procedure [5]. This approach has been employed in the characterization of the inclusion of a wide range of drugs on cyclodextrins, and also in the aggregation of host units either in dimerization [15, 48] or in rotaxanes formation [49, 50]. Other hybrid approaches [51], including quantum mechanics/molecular mechanics (QM/MM) [29] methods have also provided insight on the formation of inclusion complexes at a molecular level.

3. Using potentials of mean force to address host-guest recognition and association

Several research groups have opened the way for future progress through innovative applications of free-energy methods to physical and organic chemistry, as well as structural biology. An exhaustive account of the wide range of works published in the early years of free-energy calculations falls beyond the scope of this section. The reader is referred to Refs. [16, 52] for a full description of these efforts.

A complete thermodynamic characterization of the binding process implies the knowledge of the enthalpy and entropy of association. This is one of the key elements in identifying the stabilizing factors and in understanding how is the guest and host assemble. Standard molecular simulation methods have reproduced the absolute thermodynamic properties of binding (standard free-energy, enthalpy and entropy) between host-guest systems [53]. The absolute binding free-energy can be expressed as the sum of separate free-energy contributions corresponding to a step-by-step process describing the association process between the host and guest [5]. This can be accomplished by calculating the PMF profile along a specific reaction coordinate characterizing the association process (this reaction coordinate can be the distance between the center of mass of the host and that of the guest).

Different methodologies have been successfully applied for the calculation of the PMF profile. Among them, free-energy perturbation (FEP) [47, 50, 54, 55], thermodynamic integration (TI) [45, 47], umbrella sampling, with the weighted histogram analysis method (WHAM) [5, 56] and force constraint methods [16] are the most commonly used in the literature for chemically and biologically relevant systems. PMF calculations play a considerable role in understanding how chemical species recognize and associate. One might argue that they actually provide a more satisfactory picture of these phenomena than alchemical free-energy calculations, because they follow the molecules of interest from their free, unbound state, to the bound state of the complex. This point of view is obviously misleading, as the model reaction coordinate followed to describe association/dissociation bears certain arbitrariness. Furthermore, PMF have helped to decode complex recognition and association phenomena in thermodynamic signatures with a detailed atomic description of the underlying processes. A detailed description of the theoretical basis of PMF calculation is given in ref. [16]

The PMF, $W(\xi)$ may be interpreted as the potential that is produced by the average forces over all the configurations of a given system, in which a set of molecules is kept fixed (at a certain value of a reaction coordinate, ξ). This quantity was devised by Kirkwood [19, 32] and can be defined based on the average distribution function, $\rho(\xi)$, along the coordinate ξ, obtained from a Boltzmann weighted average,

$$\langle\rho(\xi)\rangle = \frac{\int dr \delta(\xi'(r) - \xi)\, e^{\left(\frac{-U(r)}{k_b T}\right)}}{\int dr\, e^{\left(\frac{-U(r)}{k_b T}\right)}} \tag{1}$$

$$W(\xi) = W(\xi^*) - k_B\, T ln\left[\frac{\rho\langle\xi\rangle}{\rho\langle\xi^*\rangle}\right] \tag{2}$$

where $W(\xi^*)$ and ξ^* are arbitrary reference values, $\delta(\xi'(r) - \xi)$ represents the Dirac delta function for the coordinate ξ, $U(r)$ corresponds the total energy of the system as a function of the coordinates r, and $\xi(r)$ is a function depending on the number of degrees of freedom, such as an angle, a distance or a more complex function of the cartesian coordinates of the system.

The distribution function $\rho(\xi)$ cannot be computed by standard MC or MD simulations, due to low sampling frequency in higher-energy configurations. Specific sampling techniques (non-Boltzmann sampling) have been designed for calculating the PMF along a coordinate ξ, from a MD trajectory. The umbrella sampling technique, proposed in the 1970s by Torrie and Valleau [22], is one of these approaches, and is commonly used to overcome the difficulty of sampling rare events, by modifying the potential function so that the unfavorable states are sampled appropriately.

Umbrella sampling is used to describe simulations in which an order parameter connecting the initial and final ensembles is divided into mutually overlapping regions, or windows, which are sampled using non-Boltzmann weights. To explain briefly, several independent simulations are performed in each of the imposed regions of the reaction coordinate (**Figure 1**, bottom), using a bias potential to constrain the simulations to adjacent windows. Such initial configurations are generated, each corresponding to a location wherein the guest molecule is restrained and centered at subsequent values of ξ_i, corresponding to decreasing or increasing center of mass (COM) distances from the center of the host cavity, using an umbrella biasing potential, $w(\xi)$, often of quadratic form, $w_i(\xi) = 0.5\ K(\xi - \xi_i)^2$. This restraint allows the guest molecule to sample the configurational space in a defined region along the association/dissociation coordinate. Then the biased system (**Figure 1**, middle) will sample configurations close to a defined position, z_0, even when these would not be sampled in the unbiased system. In general, the potential energy $(U(r) + w(\xi))$ is used to generate the biased simulations. The mean force, as a function of position, is calculated in each window, and the respective potentials, $W(\xi)$, are derived using an unbiasing procedure.

Statistical techniques, such as WHAM [56] are used to remove the umbrella bias and combine the local distributions, allowing free-energy to be computed (**Figure 1**, top). WHAM is the basic tool for constructing free-energy profiles from distributions derived through stratification, for which the path connecting the reference and the target states is separated into

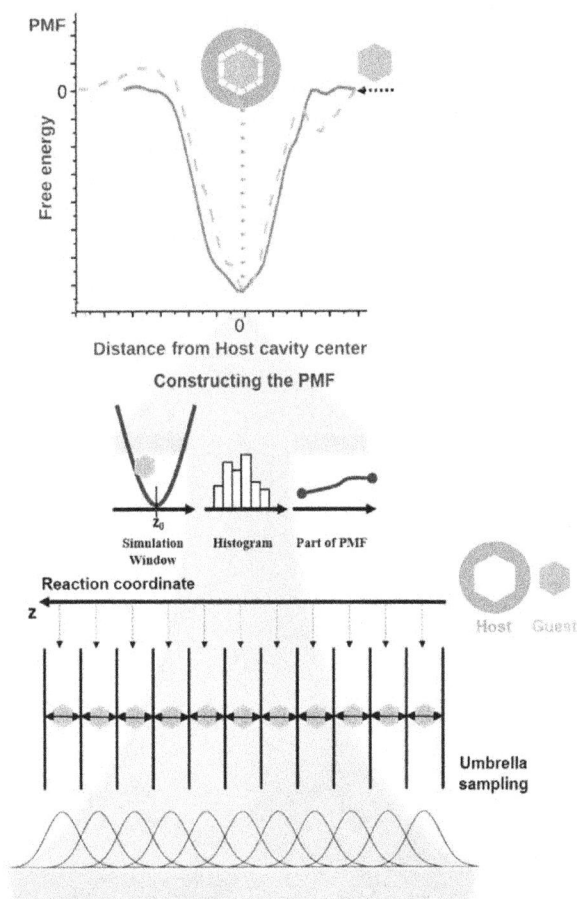

Figure 1. Schematic representation of the umbrella sampling procedure applied to a system along the pathway for the association/dissociation of a model guest with a host cavity.

intermediate states. The respective equations have also been used as the core of adaptive umbrella sampling approaches [42, 43], in which the efficiency of free-energy calculations are improved through refinement of the biasing potentials as the simulation progressed.

3.1. Thermodynamics of host-guest binding

The determination of binding affinities for host-guest complexes arising from the non-covalent association of two molecules is of paramount importance in different fields, including drug discovery. The host-guest binding affinity is related to the difference in Gibbs free energies of binding (ΔG_{bind}) corresponding to the associated and dissociated states of the system under study (see **Figure 2**).

ΔG_{bind} is composed of enthalpic and entropic terms. While the enthalpic contribution reflects changes in the inner energy of the systems, i.e. energies related to atomic motions and interactions, entropic contributions are also related with conformational changes upon binding [16].

The common methods for binding affinity estimation include very fast but less accurate similarity-based regression models and scoring functions and accurate but computationally demanding physical methods, which require a large number of MD (or Monte Carlo) simulations [57]. This suggests that the most convenient methods and algorithms are those that offer a good balance between computational costs and accuracy. Most accurate strategies provide estimates for thermodynamic quantities, with intrinsic difficulties associated to fundamental aspects. The quantification of atomic or ionic interactions, associated to repulsive and attractive forces, requires physical models assigned to different force fields (FF). The latter can be detailed using quantum mechanical (QM) *ab-initio* methods. However, a quantum mechanical representation of solvated biological systems, such as membranes and proteins consisting of large amounts of atoms is useless, even with approximations, such as the density functional theory (DFT) [58, 59]. Relevant considerations have been made [24] on the accuracy of FF for the calculation of binding thermodynamics. Some FF combinations may provide the most accurate binding enthalpies but the least accurate binding free energies, with implications in the development of new FF. These have been evaluated for a wide range of host-guest complexes and water models, using different partial charge assignment methods and host FF parameters, and resorting to the attach-pull-release (APR) method [24], which allows computing the absolute binding free energies, from a series of umbrella sampling simulations. In the

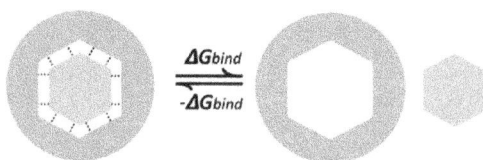

Figure 2. Schematic representations of a reversible non-covalent association/dissociation process of a guest molecule (green) and a host (orange) molecule, possessing a certain binding energy difference (ΔG_{bind}) between the associated and dissociated states.

latter, restraints controlling the host-guest complex are activated cumulatively for separating host and guest molecules, and then released to leave the guest at standard concentration.

In fact, the selection of FF and setup parameters (e.g. protonation states and slow motions) can be a difficult task, as new variants primarily concerned to the treatment of proteins, are constantly being produced. There are standard options such as OPLS [60], AMBER [61], CHARMM [62], and GROMOS [63] and other more specific FF, such as the Kirkwood-Buff [64] FF, directed at aromatic amino acids, the CHARMM polarizable FF, based on the classical Drude oscillator [65, 66], the induced dipole [67], for modeling polarization in proteins and protein-ligand complexes, the Jorgensen's approach [68] for parameterization by atoms-in-molecule electron density partitioning, AMOEBA [69] and GEM* [70], among many others [71–73]. Additionally, several water models such as TIP3P [74], TIP4Pew [75], and SPC/E [76], and the recently introduced OPC [77], TIP3P-FB and TIP4P-FB [78], TIP4P-D [79], and iAMOEBA [80] are also available. It is worth mentioning that the assessement of the ability of these FF to reproduce experimental data are very sparse, and based on the free-energy of hydration of small molecules [81], and on the structure of nucleic acids [82] and proteins [83]. With regard to explicit solvent methods, only a few studies have focused on thermodynamic data from non-covalent binding for validating the FF. Recently [84, 85], the binding free energies of cyclodextrin host-guest complexes were also used, but in the context of implicit solvent models.

It is worth to note that there are other issues in this type of systems that transcend the accuracy of the selected FF, and affect the simulation results. These are related to restrictions for the sampling and estimation of reliable thermodynamic quantities, including the respective binding constants. The latter can be determined from experimental techniques such as ^{1}H NMR, isothermal titration calorimetry and solubility experiments. The calculations of binding constants that provide a convenient counterpart to the experimental observations in inclusion complexes is sometimes addressed using a "flexible molecule" approximation [5], instead of the conventional rigid rotor harmonic oscillator [86–88]. The available volume for a guest molecule is described in terms of a cylindrical, PMF weighted region, in which the respective motion is measured by the positioning of the center of mass. The "flexible molecule" approximation is not as widespread as might be expected, and relatively recent publications [86, 89] both divulge the approximation and highlight controversies on the topic. In simple terms, the binding constant, K_{bind} can be estimated by integrating the PMF values ($\Delta G_{PMF}(\xi)$ along the association/dissociation coordinate, ξ, from

$$K_{bind} = \pi N_A \int r\,(\xi)^2\, e^{\left(\frac{-\Delta G_{PMF}(\xi)}{RT}\right)} d\xi \qquad (3)$$

where N_A and R corresponds to the Avogadro and the ideal gas constants, respectively and r is the average radius of the cross section of the cylinder in each sampling window, which is also a function of ξ.

The key factors affecting the thermodynamic signatures in host-guest systems can also be assessed along with an accurate description of the NCI including their spatial features. This can be carried out resorting to a recently developed Independent Gradient Method (IGM) of Lefebvre and co-workers [90] (see Section 4 for details), which allows the visualization of regions of low charge density corresponding to stabilizing/destabilizing NCI, based on the analysis of the electronic charge density of the interacting molecules and the respective gradients. Although the original NCI method of Johnson and co-workers [91] provide a very similar qualitative analysis of NCI, the reduced density gradient, s, used to identify the interaction types is a dimensionless quantity and therefore difficults the evaluation of the respective strengths. The new IGM allows for a quantitative comparison of the strength of NCI through the calculation of the IGM descriptor, δ_g, which corresponds directly to the charge density gradient(s) in real-space.

4. Visualizing NCI using a charge density topology

The topological features of the electronic charge density have played an important part in several schemes aiming to provide a route to understanding molecular structure from first principles, that is, without resorting to any form of empirical or approximate models (other than the physically justified approximations underlying the electronic structure methods employed). Methods such as the theory of Atoms in Molecules (AIM) [92] and the Electron Localisation Function (ELF) [93–95] can provide great insight into features of the density. Both AIM and the ELF are useful for studying strong interactions such as covalent or ionic bonding but are not as useful in the analysis of very weak interactions of the type that are important for subjects as diverse as protein structure, drug design, catalysis, materials self-assembly, and many more. To address this, Johnson et al. [91, 96] introduced the NCI analysis method. This approach is based on the electronic charge density, ρ, and its derivatives. The first derivative $\nabla\rho$ enters into the expression for the reduced density gradient, s,

$$ s = \frac{1}{(2(3\pi^2))^{1/3}} \frac{|\nabla\rho|}{\rho^{4/3}} \tag{4} $$

In regions of low ρ such as the density tails far from a molecule the gradient remains large and so s displays high values. However, in regions of low ρ between atoms where weak NCI occur the gradient (and therefore s) drop to zero.

In order to differentiate between stabilizing attractive interactions and those that are unfavorable and destabilize the system it is necessary to analyze the second derivative (Laplacian) of the charge density $\nabla^2\rho$. Decomposition of $\nabla^2\rho$ into the three eigenvalues representing the axes of maximal variation

$$ \nabla^2\rho = \lambda_1 + \lambda_2 + \lambda_3, \ (\lambda_1 \le \lambda_2 \le \lambda_3) \tag{5} $$

provides information on the nature of the interactions at a given point in space. λ_2 displays negative values in stabilizing/bonding regions (charge is flowing into this region indicating a local build-up of ρ) while in destabilizing/repulsive regions it is positive (charge flowing out, indicating a local depletion of ρ). Plotting s against $sign(\lambda_2)\rho$ will therefore permit the identification of NCI in regions where s and $sign(\lambda_2)\rho \rightarrow 0$. Although these quantities can be readily obtained with first principles electronic structure methods, such calculations remain too computationally expensive for the large systems of interest in biological or materials science applications. In such cases it is possible to approximate the charge density with a sum of atomic densities providing a pro-molecular density, ρ^{pro}. This approximate density does not include relaxation of the atomic densities as would happen in self-consistent calculations for bonded systems. Fortunately, the largest deviation of ρ^{pro} from the fully relaxed density occurs in covalent bonding regions and has a minimal effect on the (low-density) NCI regions.

Substituting ρ^{pro} into the equations above has been found to have have very little impact on the resulting NCI analysis. For purposes of interfacing with the results of molecular dynamics simulations, pro-molecular densities have the additional advantages that they are readily computed for both finite and extended/periodic systems and the fact that this approach requires orders of magnitude less computational time than the method based on first principles electronic structure calculations.

A recent development of the NCI method that makes use of the pro-molecular route to building the charge density of the system under study is the Independent Gradient Method (IGM) of Lefebvre et al. [90] As with the NCI method, IGM employs in addition to ρ quantities related to the first and second derivatives of the density. However, in IGM the reduced density gradient, s, is replaced with the descriptor δg^{inter}, defined as the difference between the first derivatives of the charge densities for the total system and the fragments

$$\delta g^{inter} = \left|\nabla\rho^{IGM,\ inter}\right| - \left|\nabla\rho\right| \tag{6}$$

$\delta g^{inter} > 0$ indicates the presence of NCI and the magnitude of the descriptor at a point in space gives an indication of the strength of the interaction. $\nabla\rho^{IGM,\ inter}$ is obtained from sums over all the atomic densities in the different fragments (here for two fragments A and B in the x-direction)

$$\left(\frac{\delta\rho}{\delta x}\right)^{IGM,inter} = \left|\sum_{i=1}^{N_A}\frac{\delta\rho_i}{\delta x}\right| + \left|\sum_{i=1}^{N_B}\frac{\delta\rho_i}{\delta x}\right| \tag{7}$$

The IGM approach has the attractive feature that δg^{inter} allows for a more facile comparison of the strength of the weak interactions than the quantity s in the original NCI [90]. This is due to the fact that the presence of significant non-covalent interactions is indicated when $s \to 0$ making interpretation difficult whereas the magnitude of the IGM quantity δg^{inter} increases in proportion to the strength of the interaction.

An illustrative example of the use of the NCI and IGM methods is given in **Figures 3** and **4**. The host-guest complex shown is between curcurbit[7]uril and the dodecyl serine-based monomeric cationic surfactant 12SerTFAc [97] (to make the example more accessible to the reader only a single configuration is shown). Calculation of the NCI and IGM descriptors was performed using IGMPlot version 1.0 (http://kisthelp.univ-reims.fr/IGMPLOT/).

As can be seen from the molecular structure images, both the s and δg^{inter} surfaces provide qualitatively similar information and display the general distribution of the most significant

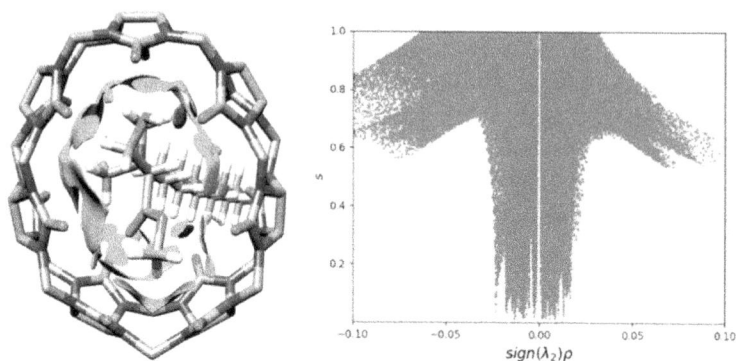

Figure 3. Host-guest complexation between curcurbit[7]uril and the dodecyl serine-based monomeric cationic surfactant 12SerTFAc. (left) reduced density gradient, $s = 0.4$, isosurface colored by value of $sign(\lambda_2)\rho$ ($-0.03 \leq sign(\lambda_2)\rho \leq 0.03$ a.U.). Blue = stabilizing, red = destabilizing and green = weak interactions. (right) scatter plot of s and $sign(\lambda_2)\rho$ values.

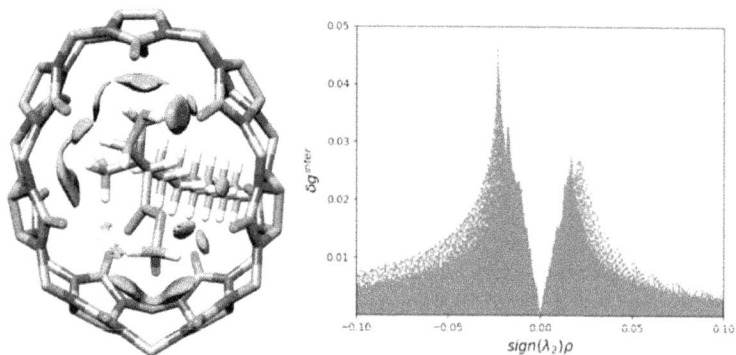

Figure 4. Host-guest complexation between curcurbit[7]uril and 12serTFAc sufactant. (left) IGM $\delta g^{inter} = 0.01$ a.U. Isosurface colored by value of $sign(\lambda_2)\rho$ ($-0.03 \leq sign(\lambda_2)\rho \leq 0.03$ a.U.). Blue = stabilizing, red = destabilizing and green = weak interactions. (right) scatter plot of δg^{inter} and $sign(\lambda_2)\rho$ values.

host-guest interactions. Similarly, the color-coding provided by the value of $sign(\lambda_2)\rho$ can be seen to predict that the interactions are largely of the weak van der Waals type with the exception of a single blue region denoting the hydrogen bond between the serine hydroxyl group and the host. A significant difference between the s and δg^{inter} surfaces is that the latter also contains information on the strength of the interactions through the volumes of the isosurface regions at a given point. The IGM approach therefore provides an important extra source of information on the nature of the interactions. The intrinsic difference between the two methods is even more clearly seen in the adjacent scatter plots. In the IGM plot (**Figure 4**, right) peaks of different magnitude corresponding to different strengths of interaction can be seen which give rise to the differing isosurface volumes. The NCI plot (**Figure 3**, right), however, displays all spikes in the non-covalent interaction region $-0.025 \leq sign(\lambda_2)\rho \leq 0.025$ in a very similar manner and makes interpretation much less easy. For this reason, despite very similar computational requirements for both methods making them equally suitable for analysis of large (ensembles of) systems such as those arising from MD simulations it is likely that the future will see the newer IGM method being used much more extensively than the original NCI one.

5. Applications

This section presents some examples in which MD or MC simulations are used for establishing the contributions of NCI (e.g. electrostatic, hydrophobic and hydrogen-bond interactions) to the free energy, in systems in which these are the main source of recognition, assembly, and stability. These include, for instance, host-guest complexes, polyelectrolytes and proteins.

MD and free-energy calculations have provided insight on relevant aspects including the effect of substituents, the role of solvation, and rationales for the conformation and thermodynamic characterization of the systems under investigation. Among several studies on the topic, available in the literature, only a few are briefly reviewed. For instance, MD simulations in water, with PMF estimation based on both TI and constraint force methods, have been used for inspecting the thermodynamic properties of binding of some inorganic ions, such as ClO_4^- and SO_4^{2-} (**Figure 5**), and ferrocenyl alkanethiols with both free and gold-surface confined β-cyclodextrins [14, 98]. In general, the association process between the host and guest molecules is analyzed along the reaction coordinate defined by the distance between the centers of mass of both host and guest, along a reference coordinate (e.g. z-axis). In these particular systems, electrostatic interactions and hydrogen bonding have played a major role on the binding process. For instance, simulations have elucidated the association mode of sulfate anion with free and grafted β-cyclodextrin (see **Figure 5**). For the latter system, a small minimum in the PMF profile (**Figure 5**, top), positioned at a larger distance relative to the cavity of surface-grafted cyclodextrin, suggested the formation of a noninclusion complex. The ion binds to the host by forming hydrogen bonds with the free-cyclodextrin portal. Also relevant is the individual energy contributions to the cyclodextrin-ion interaction, which is governed by electrostatic interactions. However, this favorable electrostaction contribution is not sufficient to compensate desolvation of the anion, considering the respective hydration energy [14].

The release and transport of drugs mediated by cyclodextrin-based carriers, have also been investigated [99] systematically using MD and free-energy calculations, showing the preferred inclusion modes of such drugs for cyclodextrins. One example (see **Figure 6**), refers to the binding of amphotericin B (AmB), which possesses two sites, within the respective prolonged macrolide, with higher binding affinity to γ-cyclodextrin. The decomposition of the PMFs into free-energy contributions have suggested that van der Waals and electrostatic interactions are the main driving forces responsible for the formation of this type of complexes [99].

Recently, some of the authors [5] have demonstrated the relevance of non-included moieties in the stability constants of several cyclodextrin-based complexes. The binding constants for naphtalene derivatives forming complexes with β-cyclodextrin were calculated (ranging from 128 to 2.1×10^4 kJ.mol^{-1}), pointing out the important effects of the substituents. Substitution of naphthalene promoted an increase in the binding constant (up to 100-fold), irrespective of the

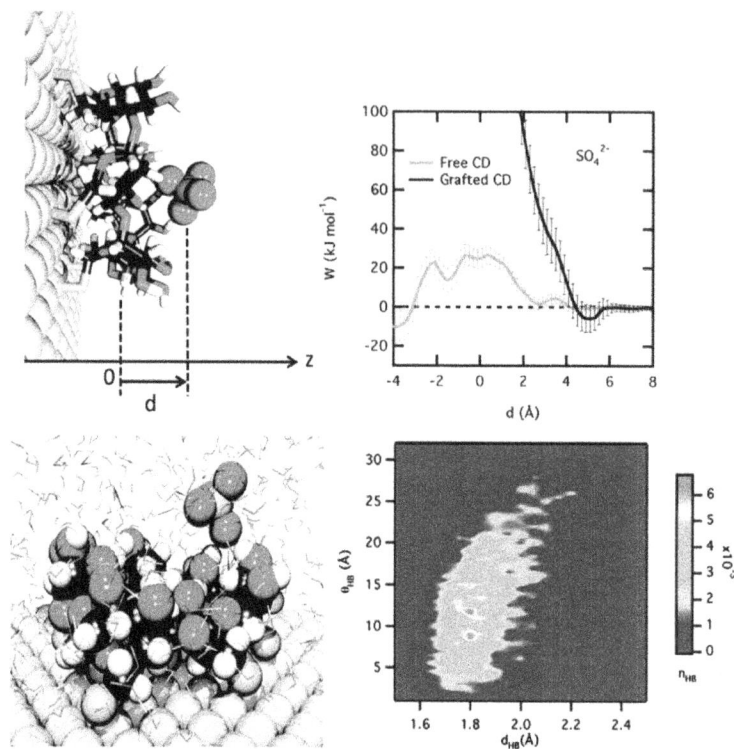

Figure 5. (Top) schematic representation of the association pathway (left) between SO_4^{2-} and a β-cyclodextrin grafted to a gold-surface, used for the construction of the PMF profile (right). The free-energy profile characterizing the association process, in water, of the ion into the free β-cyclodextrin is also shown. (Bottom) illustrative spanshot showing the presence of hydrogen bonding (right) as the ion approximates the cavity of the host, and (left) graphical distribution of distances and angles correspondonding to the hydrogen bonds. Reproduced from Ref. [14] with permission from the Royal Society of Chemistry.

nature of the substituent, the latter comprising small hydrophobic and hydrophilic, including charged, groups. Enthalpic and entropic contributions were separated in order to estimate their weight in the free-energy. Also, the preferred orientation of the guest molecules within the cyclodextrin was established.

In a completely different system [26], the same strategy was used for exploring the ion caging ability of bambusurils in aqueous media (**Figure 7**). Specifically, new insights on the conformation, hydration and energy changes involved in the complexation process between the water-soluble benzoyl-substituted bambus[6]uril and chloride ion were provided. The structural features of three single bambusuril derivatives, and the relative energy contributions to the formation of the benzoyl-substituted bambus[6]uril-chloride complex were computed. The estimated standard free-energy of binding and the respective binding constant were found to be −11.7 kJ.mol^{-1} and 112, respectively. Binding occurred with complete desolvation

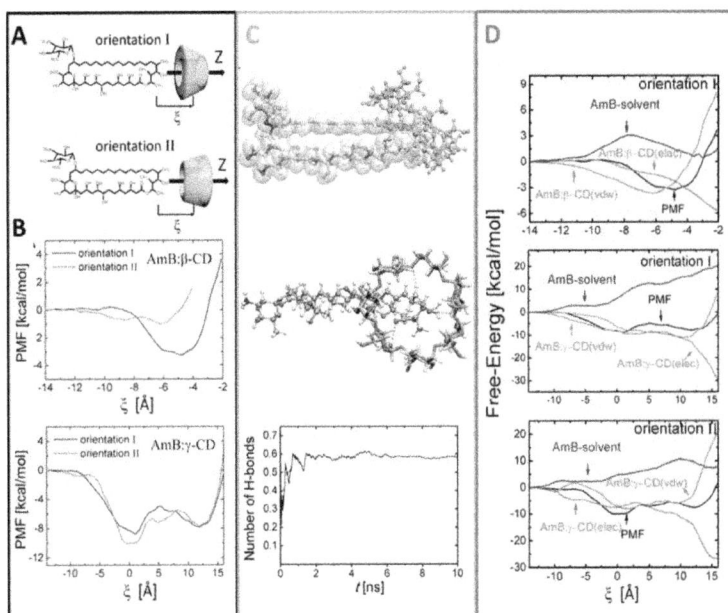

Figure 6. (A) Schematic representation of the two inclusion pathways along which AmB approximates to β- or γ-ciclodextrins. (B) PMF profiles for the inclusion of AmB with β- and γ-cyclodextrins considering the two orientations. (C) Equilibrium configuration of the complex between AmB and β-cyclodextrin (orientation I) followed by a representation of the hydrogen bonds formed between host and guest molecules and the respective averaged number (O···H···O angle >135° and O···O distance <3.5 Å), as a function of the simulation time. (D) Decomposition of the PMFs into van der Waals and electrostatic host-guest and host-solvent contributions, for the complexes between AmB and β- and γ-cyclodextrin in orientation I, and AmB and γ-cyclodextrin in orientation II. Reproduced from Ref. [99] with permission from the American Chemical Society.

of both guest and host cavity. One of the most interesting observation was that chloride was hermetically sealed inside the host cavity, as a result of a concerted action of both conformation change and desolvation (see **Figure 7**) [26].

Solvent contributions to the thermodynamics of binding have been scrutinized [13], emphasizing the importance of using explicit models for the accurate calculation of binding thermodynamics. A detailed analysis on the energetics of the host-guest complexation between β-cyclodextrin and several model drugs (e.g. puerarin, daidzin, daidzein, and nabumetone) have demonstrated that the flexibility of the binding partners and solvation-related enthalpy and entropy changes must be included explicitly for the precise estimation of thermodynamic parameters involved in molecular association. In this study, it was also demonstrated that implicit models are not suitable to provide detailed information on how free-energy is decomposed into enthalpy and entropy [13].

The dimerization of cyclodextrins has also been recognized as a relevant step in the construction of nanostructured materials. Only a few studies (see e.g. refs [15, 48].) involving umbrella

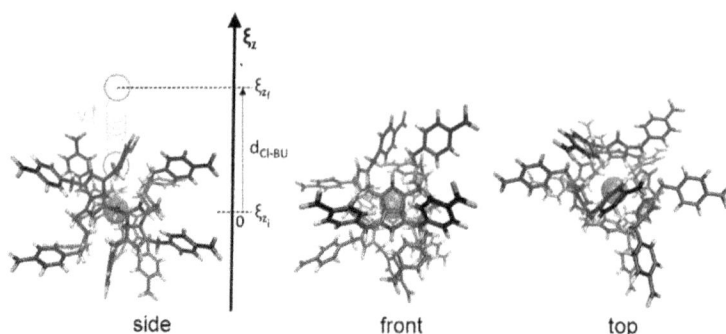

Figure 7. Typical conformation of the inclusion complex between one chloride ion (purple sphere) and the dodeca (4-carboxybenzyl)bambus[6]uril, in water, sampled during the MD run, at 298 K. (Right) Scheme of the dissociation pathway, along the z-component (ξ_z), between host and guest. The steering force is applied on the chloride ion for generating the initial configurations for the umbrella sampling procedure. Reproduced from Ref [26] with permission from Elsevier.

sampling simulations and PMF calculations have been carried out for investigating the binding affinity of dimers in the presence/absence of a guest molecule, and the preferred orientation of interglucopyranose hydrogen bonds, at the cyclodextrin portals. These include β-cyclodextrin monomers and dimers in aqueous and nonaqueous media [48]. Polar solvents with stronger hydroden bond accepting abilities can easily disrupt intermolecular hydrogen bonds, decreasing the stability of the dimers. In the same environment, higher binding affinities are achieved if guest molecules are included in the channel-type cavity of such dimers. These results allowed concluding that the formation of dimers is solvent-dependent and guest-modulated [48]. In another related study [15], it was shown that the cooperative binding of cyclodextrin cavities to guest molecules can facilitates the dimerization process, favoring the overall stability and assembly of nanostructures. Different dimerization modes yielded different binding strengths. This has been demonstrated in systems consisting of isoflavone drug analogs used as drug templates, and cyclodextrins (**Figure 8**). A detailed quantification of host, guest and solvent contributions to the thermodynamics of binding has revealed that head-to-head dimerization promotes the most stable complexes, which can be used as building blocks for template-stabilized nanostructures. Desolvation of cyclodextrin dimers and entropy changes upon complexation also affect significantly the cooperative binding [15].

Other strategies have been adopted resorting to both MD and MC simulations. As an example of application [100], free-energy calculations and lattice chain MC simulations have been used for understanding the formation of polyrotaxanes (**Figure 9**), including the identification of the most favorable conformations of cyclodextrin molecules in a polyrotaxane and the quantification of dimerization free energies, related to different spatial arrangements of two consecutive cyclodextrin molecules. It has been suggested, that the binary association is controlled by the formation of hydrogen bonds between two adjacent molecules, promoting an overall structural stabilization [100].

The thermodynamic cost of confining polyelectrolytes spherical cells of different radii can also be quantified by free-energy calculations, resorting to TI [101]. Simulation studies of

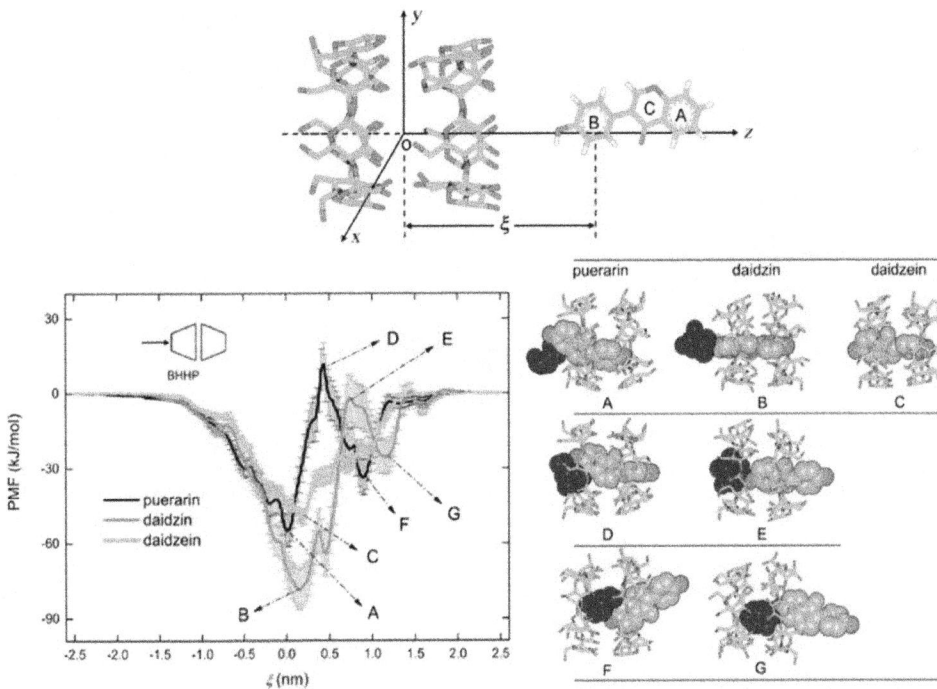

Figure 8. (Top) schematic representation of the association coordinate for the 2:1 complex between a β- cyclodextrin dimer and daidzein. (Bottom) PMF profiles and representative configurations of the 2:1 complexes between the specific BHHP arrangement of β- cyclodextrin dimer and three different model drugs. Reproduced from Ref. [15] with permission from the American Chemical Society.

polyelectrolytes, based on MC and MD, have been precluded by the respective chain lengths and the need of large concentrations of compacting agents. The conformational and energetic changes in DNA delivery systems have been studied computationally by some of the authors [101, 102]. For instance, a coarse-grained model was proposed [101] for exploring structural and thermodynamics aspects of confining polyions in spherical cavities, with different linear charge densities and with counterions of different valences. The free-energy of the confined polyion and counterions were estimated as a function of the sphere radius, from a dilute solution corresponding to the largest sphere. A positive free-energy difference was found for all systems and was associated to the compression. This means that the system containing the polyion with the largest linear charge density and monovalent counterions displays the largest resistance to being compressed. The penalty is thus largest for the polyion with the largest linear charge density and monovalent counterions. The replacement of the monovalent counterions with trivalent ones induced a compactation of the polyion, as a consequence of the stronger electrostatic polyion-counterion attraction. This leads to a nearly full compensation of the ideal and electrostatic contributions to the free-energy of their confinement.

Other interesting example of application relates to protein-ligand interactions [103–107], which are typically pursued by significant conformational and energetic changes. These

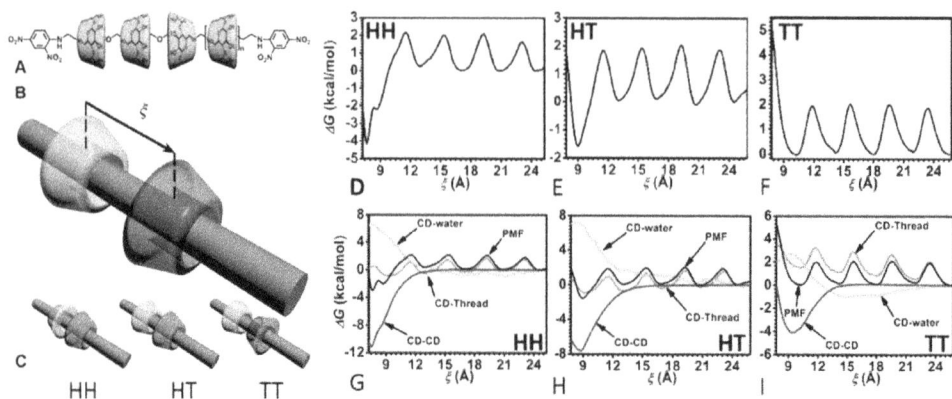

Figure 9. (A) Structural arrangement of a polyrotaxane formed formed by a poly(ethylene glycol chain included in multiple α-cyclodextrins, (B) definition of the reaction coordinate, ξ, in wich both the geometrically restrained (cyan) and free (red) cyclodextrins are presented. (C) Three possible conformations (HH, HT and TT) showing different spatial arrangements of two consecutive α-cyclodextrin molecules. (D-F) Free-energy profiles corresponding to the dimerization of α-cyclodextrins on the poly(ethylene glycol chain, for the HH, HT and TT conformations. (G-I) Individual cyclodextrin-cyclodextrin, cyclodextrin-water, and cyclodextrin-thread energy contributions for the total free-energy, in the three conformations. Reproduced from Ref. [100] with permission from the American Chemical Society.

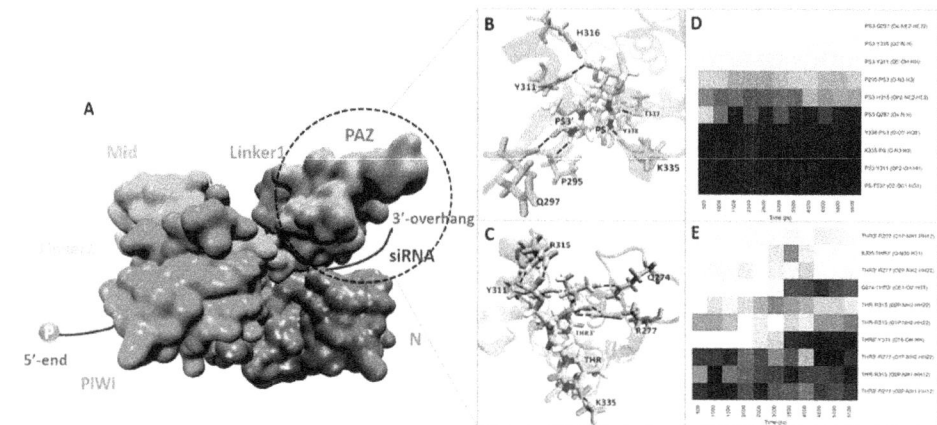

Figure 10. Representative conformation of the complex between PAZ domain of the human argonaute 2 (hAgo2) and the chemically modified siRNAs at 3' overhang, obtained from the last nanoseconds of the MD production runs. Panel A illustrates the relative positioning of domains and interdomain linker of the hAgo2 (using the crystal coordinates of PDB ID: 4F3T) and the positioning of the siRNA antisense strand. Panels **B** and **C** show the most representative structures of the complexes formed between PAZ domain and siRNAs, modified with phosphorothioate thymidine (PS) and L-threoninol-thymine (THR), respectively. PS and THR correspond to the second-last residues of the modified siRNAs while PS3' and THR3' correspond to the last one. Hydrogen-bonding interactions between the siRNA nucleotides and the PAZ amino acid residues are represented in black dash lines. The phosphorus, oxygen, nitrogen, hydrogen and sulfur atoms are colored in yellow, red, blue, white, and green respectively. Panels **D** and **E** correspond to the occupancies of the most prominent hydrogen bonds formed between the PAZ binding pocket and 2-nt modified nucleotides with PS and THR, respectively. The analysis of the instantaneous hydrogen bond formation was obtained using an in-house algorithm. Adapted from Ref. [108].

changes often occur on time scales that make direct atomic-level simulations useless. One possible alternative relies on the assumption that the change in the binding free-energy resulting, for e.g. from a mutation of a ligand bounded to a protein, complies a linear response scheme [104], with parameters estimated from training sets of protein-ligand complexes, and used for predicting binding affinities of new ligands. Another strategy is the computational design of the ligand in free and bound states. In this type of systems, the emergence of some reliable implicit solvation models and classical statistical-mechanical approaches have been part of the solution. These include, for instance, the use of the molecular mechanics Poisson-Boltzmann surface area (MM-PBSA) model [46]. A theoretical study, recently published [108], encompasses MD and free-energy calculations for evaluating the structural and thermodynamic signatures involved in the interaction of siRNA molecules, bearing chemical modifications at 3'-overhang, with the PAZ domain of human Argonaute (**Figure 10**). In these systems, a reduction of the complex binding affinity has been observed upon siRNA modification, being explained by the hampering of hydrogen bond formation in the active site of PAZ. Analyses of free-energy, achieved from simulations based on the Generalized Born and surface area continuum solvation (MM-GBSA) method, and of hydrogen bonds, have provided a complete identification of the most relevant residues for PAZ-siRNA interaction (see **Figure 10**). This data will contribute to the improved design of synthetic nucleotide analogues, circumventing some of the intrinsic siRNA drawbacks.

6. Concluding remarks

Molecular simulations, including free-energy calculations is still a fertile ground for research, from both theoretical and applied perspectives. Among the various challenges in the field of free-energy calculations, the integration of thermodynamics and kinetics through the concomitant determination of potentials of mean force and diffusivities in biased simulations, will benefit from substantial efforts. Although there is a general consensus that free-energy calculations are an important tool of computational chemistry and structural biology, thriving beyond academic walls, namely in industrial environments, some concerns still remain, dealing with the question to whether or not those methods provide convincing and reliable answers.

Acknowledgements

The authors acknowledge the Fundação para a Ciência a Tecnologia (FCT), Portuguese Agency for Scientific Research, through the Projects n. 016648 POCI-01-0145-FEDER-016648 and COMPETE POCI-01-0145-FEDER-007440. The Coimbra Chemistry Centre is also supported by FCT through the Projects PEst-OE/QUI/UI0313/2014 and POCI-01-0145-FEDER-007630. Tânia F.G.G. Cova, Sandra C. C. Nunes and Andreia. F. Jorge acknowledge, respectively, the PhD and post-doctoral research Grants SFRH/BD/95459/2013, SFRH/BPD/71683/2010 and SFRH/BPD/104544/2014, assigned by FCT.

Author details

Tânia F. Cova, Sandra C. Nunes, Bruce F. Milne, Andreia F. Jorge and Alberto C. Pais*

*Address all correspondence to: pais@qui.uc.pt

Department of Chemistry, Faculty of Science and Technology, Coimbra Chemistry Centre, CQC, University of Coimbra, Portugal

References

[1] Abel R, Wang L, Harder ED, Berne BJ, Friesner RA. Advancing drug discovery through enhanced free energy calculations. Accounts of Chemical Research. 2017;**50**:1625-1632

[2] Mobley DL, Gilson MK. Predicting binding free energies: Frontiers and benchmarks. Annual Review of Biophysics. 2017;**46**:531-558

[3] Ganesan A, Coote ML, Barakat K. Molecular dynamics-driven drug discovery: Leaping forward with confidence. Drug Discovery Today. 2017;**22**:249-269

[4] Qianqian Z, Weixiang Z, Runmiao W, Yitao W, Defang O. Research advances in molecular modeling in cyclodextrins. Current Pharmaceutical Design. 2017;**23**:522-531

[5] Cova TFGG, Nunes SCC, Pais AACC. Free-energy patterns in inclusion complexes: The relevance of non-included moieties in the stability constants. Physical Chemistry Chemical Physics. 2017;**19**:5209-5221

[6] Schneider H-J. Binding mechanisms in supramolecular complexes. Angewandte Chemie International Edition. 2009;**48**:3924-3977

[7] Biedermann F, Nau WM, Schneider H-J. The hydrophobic effect revisited—Studies with supramolecular complexes imply high-energy water as a noncovalent driving force. Angewandte Chemie International Edition. 2014;**53**:11158-11171

[8] Cova TFGG, Nunes SCC, Valente AJM, Pinho e Melo TMVD, Pais AACC. Properties and patterns in anion-receptors: A closer look at bambusurils. Journal of Molecular Liquids. 2017;**242**:640-652

[9] Abdolmaleki A, Ghasemi F, Ghasemi JB. Computer-aided drug design to explore cyclodextrin therapeutics and biomedical applications. Chemical Biology & Drug Design. 2017;**89**:257-268

[10] Schmidt BVKJ, Barner-Kowollik C. Dynamic macromolecular material design—The versatility of cyclodextrin-based host–guest chemistry. Angewandte Chemie International Edition. 2017;**56**:8350-8369

[11] Ryzhakov A, Do Thi T, Stappaerts J, Bertoletti L, Kimpe K, Sá Couto AR, Saokham P, Van den Mooter G, Augustijns P, Somsen GW, Kurkov S, Inghelbrecht S, Arien A, Jimidar MI, Schrijnemakers K, Loftsson T. Self-assembly of cyclodextrins and their complexes in aqueous solutions. Journal of Pharmaceutical Sciences. 2016;**105**:2556-2569

[12] Loh XJ. Supramolecular host-guest polymeric materials for biomedical applications. Materials Horizons. 2014;1:185-195

[13] Zhang H, Tan T, Hetényi C, van der Spoel D. Quantification of solvent contribution to the stability of noncovalent complexes. Journal of Chemical Theory and Computation. 2013;9:4542-4551

[14] Filippini G, Bonal C, Malfreyt P. How does the dehydration change the host-guest association under homogeneous and heterogeneous conditions? Physical Chemistry Chemical Physics. 2014;16:8667-8674

[15] Zhang H, Tan T, Hetényi C, Lv Y, van der Spoel D. Cooperative binding of cyclodextrin dimers to isoflavone analogues elucidated by free energy calculations. The Journal of Physical Chemistry C. 2014;118:7163-7173

[16] Chipot C, Pohorille A. Free Energy Calculations. Berlin, Heidelberg, New York: Springer; 2007

[17] Robert A, Lingle W, David LM, Richard AF. A critical review of validation, blind testing, and real- world use of alchemical protein-ligand binding free energy calculations. Current Topics in Medicinal Chemistry. 2017;17:2577-2585

[18] Chipot C. Frontiers in free-energy calculations of biological systems. Wiley Interdisciplinary Reviews: Computational Molecular Science. 2014;4:71-89

[19] Kirkwood JG. Statistical mechanics of fluid mixtures. The Journal of Chemical Physics. 1935;3:300-313

[20] Zwanzig RW. High-temperature equation of state by a perturbation method. I. Nonpolar gases. The Journal of Chemical Physics. 1954;22:1420-1426

[21] Widom B. Some topics in the theory of fluids. The Journal of Chemical Physics. 1963; 39:2808-2812

[22] Torrie GM, Valleau JP. Nonphysical sampling distributions in Monte Carlo free-energy estimation: Umbrella sampling. Journal of Computational Physics. 1977;23:187-199

[23] Bennett CH. Efficient estimation of free energy differences from Monte Carlo data. Journal of Computational Physics. 1976;22:245-268

[24] Henriksen NM, Gilson MK. Evaluating force field performance in thermodynamic calculations of cyclodextrin host-guest binding: Water models, partial charges, and host force field parameters. Journal of Chemical Theory and Computation. 2017;13:4253-4269

[25] Malhis LD, Bodoor K, Assaf KI, Al-Sakhen NA, El-Barghouthi MI. Molecular dynamics simulation of a cucurbituril based molecular switch triggered by pH changes. Computational and Theoretical Chemistry. 2015;1066:104-112

[26] Cova TFGG, Nunes SCC, Pinho e Melo TMVD, Pais AACC. Bambusurils as effective ion caging agents: Does desolvation guide conformation? Chemical Physics Letters. 2017;672:89-96

[27] Cao R, Wu S. In silico properties characterization of water-soluble γ-cyclodextrin bi-capped C60 complex: Free energy and geometrical insights for stability and solubility. Carbohydrate Polymers. 2015;**124**:188-195

[28] Cai W, Sun T, Liu P, Chipot C, Shao X. Inclusion mechanism of steroid drugs into β-cyclodextrins. Insights from free energy calculations. The Journal of Physical Chemistry B. 2009;**113**:7836-7843

[29] Sancho MI, Andujar S, Porasso RD, Enriz RD. Theoretical and experimental study of inclusion complexes of β-cyclodextrins with chalcone and 2',4'-dihydroxychalcone. The Journal of Physical Chemistry B. 2016;**120**:3000-3011

[30] Giovannelli E, Procacci P, Cardini G, Pagliai M, Volkov V, Chelli R. Binding free energies of host–guest systems by nonequilibrium alchemical simulations with constrained dynamics: Theoretical framework. Journal of Chemical Theory and Computation. 2017;**13**:5874-5886

[31] Vijayaraj R, Van Damme S, Bultinck P, Subramanian V. Molecular dynamics and umbrella sampling study of stabilizing factors in cyclic peptide-based nanotubes. The Journal of Physical Chemistry B. 2012;**116**:9922-9933

[32] Roux B. The calculation of the potential of mean force using computer simulations. Computer Physics Communications. 1995;**91**:275-282

[33] Bernardi RC, Melo MCR, Schulten K. Enhanced sampling techniques in molecular dynamics simulations of biological systems. Biochimica et Biophysica Acta (BBA) - General Subjects. 2015;**1850**:872-877

[34] Abrams C, Bussi G. Enhanced sampling in molecular dynamics using metadynamics, replica-exchange, and temperature-acceleration. Entropy. 2014;**16**:163

[35] Cavalli A, Spitaleri A, Saladino G, Gervasio FL. Investigating drug–target association and dissociation mechanisms using metadynamics-based algorithms. Accounts of Chemical Research. 2015;**48**:277-285

[36] Hamelberg D, Mongan J, McCammon JA. Accelerated molecular dynamics: A promising and efficient simulation method for biomolecules. The Journal of Chemical Physics. 2004;**120**:11919-11929

[37] Faradjian AK, Elber R. Computing time scales from reaction coordinates by milestoning. The Journal of Chemical Physics. 2004;**120**:10880-10889

[38] Bolhuis PG, Chandler D, Dellago C, Geissler PL. Transition path sampling: Throwing ropes over Rough Mountain passes, in the dark. Annual Review of Physical Chemistry. 2002;**53**:291-318

[39] Pearlman DA, Case DA, Caldwell JW, Ross WS, Cheatham TE, DeBolt S, Ferguson D, Seibel G, Kollman P. AMBER, a package of computer programs for applying molecular mechanics, normal mode analysis, molecular dynamics and free energy calculations to simulate the structural and energetic properties of molecules. Computer Physics Communications. 1995;**91**:1-41

[40] Abraham MJ, Murtola T, Schulz R, Páll S, Smith JC, Hess B, Lindahl E. GROMACS: High performance molecular simulations through multi-level parallelism from laptops to supercomputers. SoftwareX. 2015;1-2:19-25

[41] Phillips JC, Braun R, Wang W, Gumbart J, Tajkhorshid E, Villa E, Chipot C, Skeel RD, Kalé L, Schulten K. Scalable molecular dynamics with NAMD. Journal of Computational Chemistry. 2005;26:1781-1802

[42] Comer J, Gumbart JC, Hénin J, Lelièvre T, Pohorille A, Chipot C. The adaptive biasing force method: Everything you always wanted to know but were afraid to ask. The Journal of Physical Chemistry B. 2015;119:1129-1151

[43] Zhao T, Fu H, Lelièvre T, Shao X, Chipot C, Cai W. The extended generalized adaptive biasing force algorithm for multidimensional free-energy calculations. Journal of Chemical Theory and Computation. 2017;13:1566-1576

[44] Straatsma TP, Berendsen HJC. Free energy of ionic hydration: Analysis of a thermodynamic integration technique to evaluate free energy differences by molecular dynamics simulations. The Journal of Chemical Physics. 1988;89:5876-5886

[45] Martins SA, Sousa SF, Ramos MJ, Fernandes PA. Prediction of solvation free energies with thermodynamic integration using the general amber force field. Journal of Chemical Theory and Computation. 2014;10:3570-3577

[46] Genheden S, Ryde U. The MM/PBSA and MM/GBSA methods to estimate ligand-binding affinities. Expert Opinion on Drug Discovery. 2015;10:449-461

[47] He J, Chipot C, Shao X, Cai W. Cooperative recruitment of amphotericin B mediated by a cyclodextrin dimer. The Journal of Physical Chemistry C. 2014;118:24173-24180

[48] Zhang H, Tan T, Feng W, van der Spoel D. Molecular recognition in different environments: β-cyclodextrin dimer formation in organic solvents. The Journal of Physical Chemistry B. 2012;116:12684-12693

[49] Loethen S, Kim JM, Thompson DH. Biomedical applications of cyclodextrin based polyrotaxanes. Polymer Reviews. 2007;47:383-418

[50] Yu Y, Cai W, Chipot C, Sun T, Shao X. Spatial arrangement of α-cyclodextrins in a rotaxane. Insights from free-energy calculations. The Journal of Physical Chemistry B. 2008;112:5268-5271

[51] Masatake S, Fumio H. Predicting the binding free energy of the inclusion process of 2-hydroxypropyl- β -cyclodextrin and small molecules by means of the MM/3D-RISM method. Journal of Physics: Condensed Matter. 2016;28:384002

[52] Kollman P. Free energy calculations: Applications to chemical and biochemical phenomena. Chemical Reviews. 1993;93:2395-2417

[53] Ghoufi A, Malfreyt P. Calculation of the absolute thermodynamic properties of association of host-guest systems from the intermolecular potential of mean force. The Journal of Chemical Physics. 2006;125:224503

[54] Lamb ML, Jorgensen WL. Computational approaches to molecular recognition. Current Opinion in Chemical Biology. 1997;**1**:449-457

[55] Cai W, Sun T, Shao X, Chipot C. Can the anomalous aqueous solubility of [small beta]-cyclodextrin be explained by its hydration free energy alone? Physical Chemistry Chemical Physics. 2008;**10**:3236-3243

[56] Hub JS, de Groot BL, van der Spoel D. g_wham—A free weighted histogram analysis implementation including robust error and autocorrelation estimates. Journal of Chemical Theory and Computation. 2010;**6**:3713-3720

[57] Brandsdal BO, Österberg F, Almlöf M, Feierberg I, Luzhkov VB, Åqvist J. Free Energy Calculations and Ligand Binding, Advances in Protein Chemistry. Uppsala, Sweeden: Academic Press; 2003. pp. 123-158

[58] DiLabio GA, Otero-de-la-Roza A. Noncovalent Interactions in Density Functional Theory, Reviews in Computational Chemistry. Hoboken, New Jersey: John Wiley & Sons, Inc; 2016. pp. 1-97

[59] Simons J. An experimental chemist's guide to ab initio quantum chemistry. The Journal of Physical Chemistry. 1991;**95**:1017-1029

[60] Robertson MJ, Tirado-Rives J, Jorgensen WL. Improved peptide and protein torsional energetics with the OPLS-AA force field. Journal of Chemical Theory and Computation. 2015;**11**:3499-3509

[61] ITADREDTJDA Case, Betz RM, Botello-Smith W, Cerutti DS, Cheatham TE, AMBER. 16, University of California; 2016

[62] Vanommeslaeghe K, Hatcher E, Acharya C, Kundu S, Zhong S, Shim J, Darian E, Guvench O, Lopes P, Vorobyov I, Mackerell AD. CHARMM general force field: A force field for drug-like molecules compatible with the CHARMM all-atom additive biological force fields. Journal of Computational Chemistry. 2010;**31**:671-690

[63] Reif MM, Hünenberger PH, Oostenbrink C. New interaction parameters for charged amino acid side chains in the GROMOS force field. Journal of Chemical Theory and Computation. 2012;**8**:3705-3723

[64] Ploetz EA, Smith PE. A Kirkwood-buff force field for the aromatic amino acids. Physical Chemistry Chemical Physics. 2011;**13**:18154-18167

[65] Baker CM, Anisimov VM, MacKerell AD. Development of CHARMM polarizable force field for nucleic acid bases based on the classical Drude oscillator model. The Journal of Physical Chemistry B. 2011;**115**:580-596

[66] Lemkul JA, MacKerell AD. Balancing the interactions of Mg2+ in aqueous solution and with nucleic acid moieties for a polarizable force field based on the classical Drude oscillator model. The Journal of Physical Chemistry B. 2016;**120**:11436-11448

[67] Wang Z-X, Zhang W, Wu C, Lei H, Cieplak P, Duan Y. Strike a balance: Optimization of backbone torsion parameters of AMBER polarizable force field for simulations of proteins and peptides. Journal of Computational Chemistry. 2006;**27**:781-790

[68] Cole DJ, Vilseck JZ, Tirado-Rives J, Payne MC, Jorgensen WL. Biomolecular force field parameterization via atoms-in-molecule electron density partitioning. Journal of Chemical Theory and Computation. 2016;**12**:2312-2323

[69] Shi Y, Xia Z, Zhang J, Best R, Wu C, Ponder JW, Ren P. Polarizable atomic multipole-based AMOEBA force field for proteins. Journal of Chemical Theory and Computation. 2013;**9**:4046-4063

[70] Duke RE, Starovoytov ON, Piquemal J-P, Cisneros GA. GEM*: A molecular electronic density-based force field for molecular dynamics simulations. Journal of Chemical Theory and Computation. 2014;**10**:1361-1365

[71] Grimme S. A general quantum mechanically derived force field (QMDFF) for molecules and condensed phase simulations. Journal of Chemical Theory and Computation. 2014;**10**:4497-4514

[72] Monti S, Corozzi A, Fristrup P, Joshi KL, Shin YK, Oelschlaeger P, van Duin ACT, Barone V. Exploring the conformational and reactive dynamics of biomolecules in solution using an extended version of the glycine reactive force field. Physical Chemistry Chemical Physics. 2013;**15**:15062-15077

[73] Gao J, Truhlar DG, Wang Y, Mazack MJM, Löffler P, Provorse MR, Rehak P. Explicit polarization: A quantum mechanical framework for developing next generation force fields. Accounts of Chemical Research. 2014;**47**:2837-2845

[74] Jorgensen WL, Chandrasekhar J, Madura JD, Impey RW, Klein ML. Comparison of simple potential functions for simulating liquid water. The Journal of Chemical Physics. 1983;**79**:926-935

[75] Horn HW, Swope WC, Pitera JW, Madura JD, Dick TJ, Hura GL, Head-Gordon T. Development of an improved four-site water model for biomolecular simulations: TIP4P-Ew. The Journal of Chemical Physics. 2004;**120**:9665-9678

[76] Berendsen HJC, Grigera JR, Straatsma TP. The missing term in effective pair potentials. The Journal of Physical Chemistry. 1987;**91**:6269-6271

[77] Izadi S, Anandakrishnan R, Onufriev AV. Building Water Models: A Different Approach. The Journal of Physical Chemistry Letters. 2014;**5**:3863-3871

[78] Wang L-P, Martinez TJ, Pande VS. Building force fields: An automatic, systematic, and reproducible approach. The Journal of Physical Chemistry Letters. 2014;**5**:1885-1891

[79] Piana S, Donchev AG, Robustelli P, Shaw DE. Water dispersion interactions strongly influence simulated structural properties of disordered protein states. The Journal of Physical Chemistry B. 2015;**119**:5113-5123

[80] Wang L-P, Head-Gordon T, Ponder JW, Ren P, Chodera JD, Eastman PK, Martinez TJ, Pande VS. Systematic improvement of a classical molecular model of water. The Journal of Physical Chemistry B. 2013;**117**:9956-9972

[81] Mobley DL, Bayly CI, Cooper MD, Shirts MR, Dill KA. Small molecule hydration free energies in explicit solvent: An extensive test of fixed-charge atomistic simulations. Journal of Chemical Theory and Computation. 2009;**5**:350-358

[82] Galindo-Murillo R, Robertson JC, Zgarbová M, Šponer J, Otyepka M, Jurečka P, Cheatham TE. Assessing the current state of amber force field modifications for DNA. Journal of Chemical Theory and Computation. 2016;**12**:4114-4127

[83] Maier JA, Martinez C, Kasavajhala K, Wickstrom L, Hauser KE, Simmerling C. ff14SB: Improving the accuracy of protein side chain and backbone parameters from ff99SB. Journal of Chemical Theory and Computation. 2015;**11**:3696-3713

[84] Wickstrom L, He P, Gallicchio E, Levy RM. Large scale affinity calculations of cyclodextrin host–guest complexes: Understanding the role of reorganization in the molecular recognition process. Journal of Chemical Theory and Computation. 2013;**9**:3136-3150

[85] Zhang H, Yin C, Yan H, van der Spoel D. Evaluation of generalized born models for large scale affinity prediction of cyclodextrin host–guest complexes. Journal of Chemical Information and Modeling. 2016;**56**:2080-2092

[86] Zhou H-X, Gilson MK. Theory of free energy and entropy in noncovalent binding. Chemical Reviews. 2009;**109**:4092-4107

[87] Yang T, Wu JC, Yan C, Wang Y, Luo R, Gonzales MB, Dalby KN, Ren P. Virtual screening using molecular simulations. Proteins. 2011;**79**:1940-1951

[88] Suarez D, Diaz N. Conformational and entropy analyses of extended molecular dynamics simulations of [small alpha]-, [small beta]- and [gamma]-cyclodextrins and of the [small beta]-cyclodextrin/nabumetone complex. Physical Chemistry Chemical Physics. 2017;**19**:1431-1440

[89] De Jong DH, Schäfer LV, De Vries AH, Marrink SJ, Berendsen HJC, Grubmüller H. Determining equilibrium constants for dimerization reactions from molecular dynamics simulations. Journal of Computational Chemistry. 2011;**32**:1919-1928

[90] Lefebvre C, Rubez G, Khartabil H, Boisson J-C, Contreras-Garcia J, Henon E. Accurately extracting the signature of intermolecular interactions present in the NCI plot of the reduced density gradient versus electron density. Physical Chemistry Chemical Physics. 2017;**19**:17928-17936

[91] Contreras-García J, Johnson ER, Keinan S, Chaudret R, Piquemal J-P, Beratan DN, Yang W. NCIPLOT: A program for plotting noncovalent interaction regions. Journal of Chemical Theory and Computation. 2011;**7**:625-632

[92] Bader RFW. Atoms in Molecules: A Quantum Theory. Oxford: Clarendon Press; 1994

[93] Becke AD, Edgecombe KE. A simple measure of electron localization in atomic and molecular systems. The Journal of Chemical Physics. 1990;**92**:5397-5403

[94] Silvi B, Savin A. Classification of chemical bonds based on topological analysis of electron localization functions. Nature. 1994;**371**:683

[95]   Burnus T, Marques MAL, Gross EKU. Time-dependent electron localization function. Physical Review A. 2005;**71**:010501

[96]   Johnson ER, Keinan S, Mori-Sánchez P, Contreras-García J, Cohen AJ, Yang W. Revealing noncovalent interactions. Journal of the American Chemical Society. 2010;**132**:6498-6506

[97]   Brito RO, Silva SG, Fernandes RMF, Marques EF, Enrique-Borges J, do Vale MLC. Enhanced interfacial properties of novel amino acid-derived surfactants: Effects of headgroup chemistry and of alkyl chain length and unsaturation. Colloids and Surfaces B: Biointerfaces. 2011;**86**:65-70

[98]   Filippini G, Goujon F, Bonal C, Malfreyt P. Host–guest complexation in the ferrocenyl alkanethiols–Thio β-cyclodextrin mixed self-assembled monolayers. The Journal of Physical Chemistry C. 2014;**118**:3102-3109

[99]   He J, Chipot C, Shao X, Cai W. Cyclodextrin-mediated recruitment and delivery of amphotericin B. The Journal of Physical Chemistry C. 2013;**117**:11750-11756

[100] Liu P, Chipot C, Shao X, Cai W. How do α-cyclodextrins self-organize on a polymer chain? The Journal of Physical Chemistry C. 2012;**116**:17913-17918

[101] Pais AACC, Miguel MG, Linse P, Lindman B. Polyelectrolytes confined to spherical cavities. The Journal of Chemical Physics. 2002;**117**:1385-1394

[102] Dias R, Lindman B. DNA Interactions with Polymers and Surfactants. Hoboken, New Jersey: John Wiley & Sons; 2008

[103] Vettoretti G, Moroni E, Sattin S, Tao J, Agard DA, Bernardi A, Colombo G. Molecular dynamics simulations reveal the mechanisms of allosteric activation of Hsp90 by designed ligands. Scientific Reports. 2016;**6**:23830

[104] Khandelwal A, Balaz S. Improved estimation of ligand-macromolecule binding affinities by linear response approach using a combination of multi-mode MD simulation and QM/MM methods. Journal of Computer-Aided Molecular Design. 2007;**21**:131-137

[105] Abriata LA, Dal Peraro M. Assessing the potential of atomistic molecular dynamics simulations to probe reversible protein-protein recognition and binding. Scientific Reports. 2015;**5**:10549

[106] Childers MC, Daggett V. Insights from molecular dynamics simulations for computational protein design. Molecular Systems Design & Engineering. 2017;**2**:9-33

[107] Kuhn B, Tichý M, Wang L, Robinson S, Martin RE, Kuglstatter A, Benz J, Giroud M, Schirmeister T, Abel R, Diederich F, Hert J. Prospective evaluation of free energy calculations for the prioritization of Cathepsin L inhibitors. Journal of Medicinal Chemistry. 2017;**60**:2485-2497

[108] Alagia A, Jorge AF, Avino A, Cova TF, Crehuet R, Grijalvo S, Pais AC, Eritja R. Exploring PAZ/3′-overhang interaction to improve siRNA specificity. A combined experimental and modeling study. Chemical Science. 2018;**9**:2074-2086

Chapter 3

Atomic Mechanisms Governing Strength of Metallic Nanosized Crystals

Sergiy Kotrechko, Olexandr Ovsijannikov,
Igor Mikhailovskij and Nataliya Stetsenko

Additional information is available at the end of the chapter

http://dx.doi.org/10.5772/intechopen.75159

Abstract

Fundamentals of the atomic mechanisms governing the strength of nanosized metallic crystals are described. An attempt is made to explain on this basis the size and orientation effects, temperature dependence of strength and atomism of fracture of bcc crystals under triaxial uniform (hydrostatic) tension. A feature of the proposed material is that it combines the results of molecular dynamics simulation with the data of experimental research findings on failure of metallic nanosized crystals under the high-field mechanical loading. It is exhibited that local instability of the lattice is the main mechanism governing the strength of defect-free nanosized crystals (NSC). Based on the concept of local instability, an explanation is given of the nature of the size effect in NSC, as well as of the differences in its manifestation in nanocrystals with bcc and fcc lattices. The concept of the mechanism of thermal activation of local instability is outlined. This enables to explain the specific features of the temperature dependence of NSC. The results of experimental studies and molecular dynamics simulation of the failure of tungsten nanocrystals under hydrostatic tension are presented. The ideas about the atomism of the bcc-fcc transition in these conditions are articulated.

Keywords: molecular dynamic simulation, nanosized crystals, lattice instability, strength, nanowire, size effect, surface tension

1. Introduction

Significant advances in the fabrication of nanoscale objects with controlled size and properties (nanorods, nanowires, nanopillars and carbyne chains) are a characteristic feature of nanotechnology development in the last decade. In turn, this stimulates the development of experimental methods for characterising the properties of these nanoobjects, as well as computer methods for predicting their behaviour under various external influences. Nanosized metallic crystals occupy a special place among these objects. Due to their remarkable physical and mechanical properties, they can be directly used in various nanodevices; in addition, they are considered as building blocks for the creation of nanocrystalline materials. On the other hand, study of nanosized crystals enables to ascertain the fundamental mechanisms of deformation and fracture inherent in the nanoscale. Fabrication of defect-free nanocrystals and their compression test [1–3], as well as the development of a high-field technique for the preparation and *in-situ* tensile testing of nanoneedles [4–6], becomes a milestone event in experimental studies of nanosized crystals. Absence of defects (dislocations and twins) in these crystals made it possible to reach extremely high levels of strength, which are close to the value of "theoretical strength". Therefore, molecular dynamics (MD) simulation is the most effective tool for studying atomic mechanisms to reach extremely high levels of strength in crystals.

Nanosized crystals of bcc metals are a classical object of MD simulation [7–13]. Currently, considerable attention is paid to metals with a bcc lattice [14–20]. From a physical point of view, bcc metals are more interesting because they provide a greater variety of atomic rearrangements, governing the strength. However, the main difficulty in MD simulation of bcc metal is lack of sufficiently reliable potentials, which limits the accuracy of such simulation. In this connection, the appearance of direct experimental data on the strength of bcc nanocrystals substantially facilitated the problem of selection and verification of these potentials. A great number of works on MD-simulation enabled to predict the key effects controlling the level of strength of nanosized nanocrystals, namely: (i) the size effect, (ii) dependence of strength on orientation, (iii) the temperature dependence of strength, and (iv) dependence of strength on the stress state mode [7–24]. At the same time, the absence of a completed theory of strength of nanosized crystals is a characteristic feature of science of the strength of these objects. Lack of sufficient experimental data is the second feature of state-of-the-art in researches of strength of nanosized crystals. Difficulties in performing mechanical tests of nanospecimens are the reason for this. In this regard, the high-field mechanical tests of nanosized specimens should be indicated. It has made it possible *in situ* mechanical loading of nanosized specimens up to level close to theoretical strength combined with direct observation of the atomic structure of these objects under well-controlled crystallographic conditions [25, 26].

In the present work, fundamentals of the atomic mechanisms governing strength of nanosized metallic crystals are described; besides, an attempt is made to explain on this basis the size and orientation effects, temperature dependence of strength, and atomism of fracture of bcc crystals under triaxial uniform (hydrostatic) tension.

2. Methods of physical and numerical experiments

2.1. Field-induced mechanical test

The *in situ* mechanical loading of nanosized crystals in the FIM experiments was realised using the Maxwell mechanical stress induced by high electric fields. As was shown in these studies, the vast majority of dislocations was removed under the action of the electric field–induced mechanical stresses. So, most of the dislocation-free nanosized crystals were fractured at mechanical stresses corresponded to substantial parts of the ideal strength of solids. This technique was used for uniaxial tensile tests of tungsten and molybdenum nanoneedles and for uniform triaxial (hydrostatic) tensile tests of a tungsten nanocrystal.

The intrinsic hydrostatic tensile strength of tungsten was experimentally determined using a high-field testing in field-ion microscope (FIM) with needle-shaped specimens (**Figure 1a**) [6]. The specimens with an initial radius of curvature of about 100 nm and the taper angle of $5 - 15°$ were etching in a NaOH solution of 99.98% pure tungsten wires with the <110> texture. The specimen surface was preliminary polished by low-temperature field evaporation [25]. Field ion images were acquired at the voltage of 4–22 kV. For mechanical loading, a high voltage pulse V_p with duration of 20 ns was applied. The local field at specimen surface was determined as

$$F = \frac{F_0 \times (V_0 + V_p)}{V_0}, \tag{1}$$

where V_0 is the applied voltage corresponding to the threshold field for evaporation F_0 [25, 27]. The evaporation field of tungsten F_0 on the [110] facets at 77 K is 57 V nm^{-1} related to an evaporation rate of ~10^{-2} atomic layers per second. The electric field decreases severely under

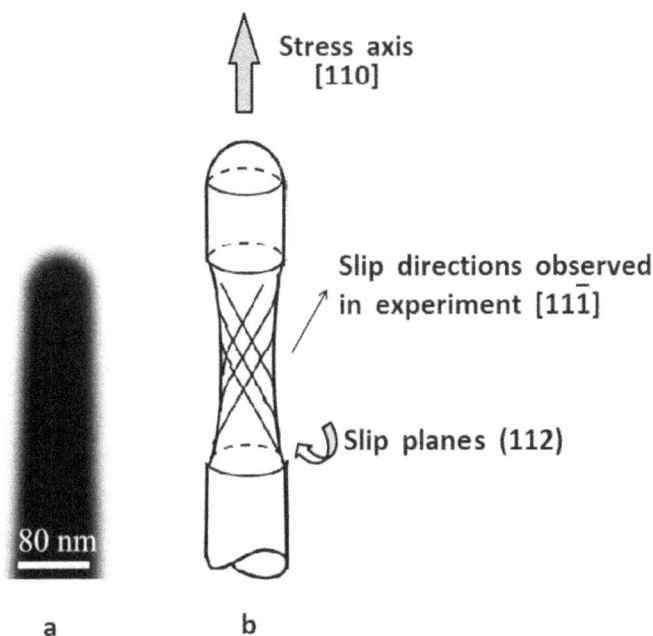

a   b

Figure 1. An electron microscopic image of Mo nanotip formed by field evaporation (a) and the sketch of a high-field tension test (b).

the hemispherical cap in the conical part. So, the failure of needle-shaped specimens was usually initiated at the nanosized cap in the region of the ultimate field strength. An electric field applied to a metal specimen induces the Maxwell surface stress

$$\sigma_s = \frac{\varepsilon_0 F^2}{2} \qquad (2)$$

where ε_0 is the electric constant. This stress acts normal to the surface element at all points. The stress state of a needle-shaped specimen is possible to estimate to any plane in the specimen apex section by integration of the stress components at each point on the surface. The Maxwell stress acting over the metal surface produces the force in the axis direction is given by:

$$f_z = \frac{1}{2}\iint \varepsilon_0 F^2 \cos\beta dS, \qquad (3)$$

where dS is an element of surface area, β is the angle between the axis and the normal to that surface facet. The integral is taken over the whole specimen surface. The local Maxwell stress is calculated by integration of the field-induced stress and dividing by the area of the section concerned. The near surface Maxwell stress under the hemispherical envelope of the specimen is virtually hydrostatic and equals to the local surface stress determined by Eq. (3). The stress state in the conical shank region is corresponded to the tensile test with uniaxial tension. It enables both to deform nanocrystal plastically and to break it under uniaxial tension (**Figure 1b**).

For nanocrystal failure under multiaxial uniform (hydrostatic) tension, a protrusion was formed on the spherical part of specimen. It was created by selection of special schedules for the high-field evaporation of atoms from the nanospecimen surface [19]. This is shown schematically in **Figure 2a**. Electric field strength and, accordingly, mechanical stresses increase with decrease in the curvature radius of a surface. So, maximal stresses act in this protrusion. This makes it possible to fracture the metal exactly in this volume. It is done by a steep increase in the electric field strength. Appearance of the crater on a nanoneedle surface is the direct evidence that fracture *occurs* in the local region, where hydrostatic tension acts (**Figure 2b**).

The Maxwell stress was determined with accuracy of ±4%. The systematic error due to uncertainties in the field calibration is ±3% (see [28, 29]), and, correspondingly, the systematic error in determination of the Maxwell stress is ±6%. The total error in determination of the Maxwell stress is ±10%.

2.2. Molecular dynamics simulation

To analyse atomic mechanisms of instability and failure of defect-free nanosized crystal under uniform triaxial (hydrostatic) tension, MD simulation was employed. Simulation was performed using the software (program package) XMD [http://xmd.sourceforge.net/].

Extended Finnis–Sinclair semiempirical potential [30] (**Tables 1 and 2**) was utilised for MD simulation of hydrostatic tension of tungsten. This potential overcomes the "soft" behaviour of the original Finnis–Sinclair potential [31].

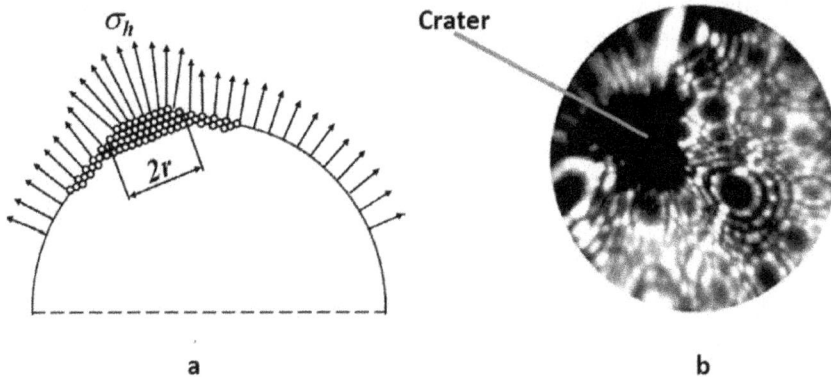

Figure 2. The schemes of the nanoneedle tip and loading (r is the protrusion radius) *before failure* (a) and FIM microfractograms of tungsten nanotip acquired at 5.60 kV *immediately after failure* (b).

A, (eV A^{-1})	d, A	c, (A)	c_0, (eV A^{-2})	c_1, (eV A^{-3})	c_2, (eV A^{-4})	c_3, (eV A^{-5})	c_4, (eV A^{-6})
1.885948	4.41	3.25	48.527 96	−33.79621	5.854334	−0.0098221	0.033338

Table 1. Potential parameters for W.

A, (eV A^{-1})	d, A	c, (A)	c_0, (eV A^{-2})	c_1, (eV A^{-3})	c_2, (eV A^{-4})	c_3, (eV A^{-5})	c_4, (eV A^{-6})
1.848648	4.1472	3.2572	47.98066	−34.09924	5.832293	0.017494	0.020393

Table 2. Potential parameters for Mo.

According to EAM or FS formalism, the total energy of a system is given by the expression:

$$U_{tot} = \frac{1}{2}\sum_{ij} V(r_{ij}) + \sum_i f(\rho_i) \tag{4}$$

where the first term is the conventional central pair-potential summation:

$$V(r) = \begin{cases} (r-c)^2 (c_0 + c_1 r + c_2 r^2 + c_3 r^3 + c_4 r^4), & r \leq c \\ 0, & r > c \end{cases}$$

and the second term is the n-body term:

$$f(\rho_i) = \sqrt{\rho_i} \quad \rho_i = \sum_{i \neq j} A^2 \varphi(r_{ij})$$

$$\varphi(r) = \begin{cases} (r-d)^2, & r \leq d \\ 0, & r > d \end{cases}$$

Uniform triaxial tension of ball-shaped nanosized tungsten crystal was also simulated. Initial radius of nanocrystal was 10.8 nm. Such a size enabled to eliminate the influence of rigid surface shell on the behaviour of atoms in the inner region of specimen. To describe the distribution of atomic velocities for given temperature, the Boltzmann distribution was used. To hold simulated temperatures, velocity of atoms was scaled by $(T_t/T_c)^{1/33}$ (T_t is the value of temperature kept during simulation; T_c is the instantaneous system temperature at each time step). To avoid a shock wave when loading, gradient velocity is added to interior atoms [32]. Thermal motion of the atoms of the surface layer of a thickness 0.5 nm was "frozen." These atoms had only the radial component of the velocity, which ensured uniform triaxial expansion of the ball shell with the rate 5 m/s. Accordingly, the strain rate was $4.63 \times 10^8\,\mathrm{s}^{-1}$. Tension of nanowires of molybdenum and tungsten in three crystallographic directions [100], [110] and [111] was modelled also. Cylinder with the axis oriented along a corresponding crystallographic direction was cut from the set of atoms placed exactly at a lattice site. Relation between the diameter and the length of cylinder is one-quarter. After that, boundary conditions are applied. The central part (gauge length) of the cylinder with length of 3 diameters is still free, but atoms of border parts are made "frozen." Time step is 10^{-15} sec. The diameter of nanospecimens varied within the range 1÷13 nm. In addition, to interpret the experimental data on the destruction of nanopillars under uniaxial compression, MD simulation of the compression of cylindrical Mo specimens in the [100] direction was performed.

For the quantitative analysis of the driving forces of atomic rearrangements, in addition to global stresses σ_{ij} (average over the specimen), local ξ_{ij} stresses (acting within the volume per atom) were estimated. The local stresses ξ_{ij} were determined as:

$$\xi_{ij}^k = \frac{1}{2\Omega^k} \sum_{m(\neq k)}^{n} f_i^{km} r_j^{km}. \tag{5}$$

where k refers to the considered atom; m refers to the neighbouring atom; f_i^{km} is the force vector between atoms k and m determined as the gradient of energy functional; r_j^{km} is the position vector between atoms k and m; n is the number of the nearest neighbouring atoms; Ω^k is the atomic volume; and i, j are the stress tensor indexes.

An expression for the global stresses σ_{ij} is the following:

$$\sigma_{ij} = \frac{1}{N} \sum_{k=1}^{N} \xi_{ij}^k. \tag{6}$$

where N is the total number of atoms in the nanowire.

For calculation of the local shear stresses, the following formula was used:

$$\xi_{ns} = \sum_{i,j} \xi_{ij} n_i s_j \tag{7}$$

where n_i is the normal vector for the glide plane, s_j is the slip direction.

True strain value was employed as a measure of longitudinal strain of the nanowire as a whole:

$$e_{xx} = \ln\left(1 + \frac{\Delta l_{xx}}{l_0}\right) \qquad (8)$$

where l_0 and Δl_{xx} are the initial gauge length of a specimen and its increment, respectively.

When modelling hydrostatic tension of a nanosized ball-shape specimen, engineering strain value was determined as:

$$e = \frac{\Delta r}{r_0} \qquad (9)$$

where r_0 and Δr are the initial values of radius of ball and its increment, respectively.

3. Results and discussion

As it is known, microscopic defects (dislocations and twins) are the main reason for decrease in strength of materials. Modern nanotechnologies enable us to create materials, which, in most cases, are defect-free. Therefore, initially, it was believed that their strength must tend to the ideal strength and be the intrinsic material trait much like the elastic constants. However, it was appeared that the strength of nanosized crystals changes within the wide range depending on their sizes, temperature, loading condition, etc. However, the concept of "ideal strength" can be used as a starting point for the analysis of *atomic mechanisms* governing the strength of nanosized crystals. The ideal strength of a material is defined to be the maximal *homogenous* stress that an ideal crystal can withstand. Reaching of the limit state of such crystal is related to uniform and simultaneous break of atomic bonds or its reformation. In general case, two instability modes exist for metals, namely (i) instability of crystal under the tensile stresses (instability on the Bain path for bcc crystals) and (ii) shear instability. The first mode of instability of an ideal crystal results in its disintegration. Shear instability gives rise to change in shape and orientation of an ideal crystal [33–35].

A fundamental difference of nanosized crystals from the ideal ones is that the nanocrystals can be defect-free but not ideal since the ideal position of atoms in the crystal lattice is disturbed by both (i) action of surface tension forces and (ii) thermal vibrations of atoms. Action of the surface tension forces leads to inhomogeneous distribution of local stresses. Thermal vibration of atoms causes local stress fluctuations. These two factors are the main reasons for *localisation* of process of breaking and reformation of atomic bonds in nanosized crystals [36, 37]. As a result, the above two modes of an ideal lattice instability occur in a nanosized crystal, but this instability is realised in a limited local region of the crystal. This gives rise to the fact that defects form as a result of above instability. For instance, formation of dislocations and twins is a direct consequence of this localised shear instability. The key difference of these defects from those in macrosized single crystals lies in the fact that they are *highly* non-equilibrium, since they are formed in a defect-free crystal at stresses much exceeding the critical stress of their

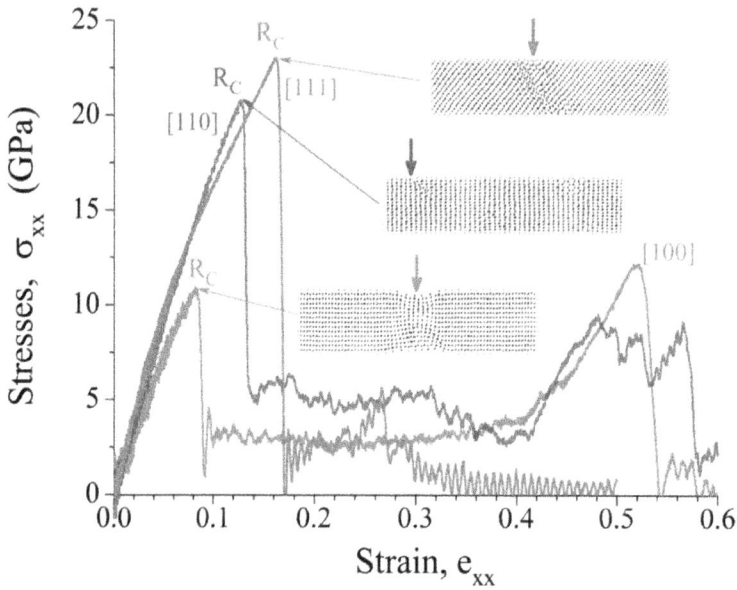

Figure 3. Images of Fe-nanowires and diagrams of their strain at temperature 300K for three crystallographic orientations: arrows indicate instability regions; R_C is the instability stress (strength of nanowire).

propagation in a crystal (**Figure 3**). As shown in **Figure 3**, the stress of formation for these defects predetermines the level of strength of nanosized crystals [37].

3.1. The effect of surface

A characteristic feature of nanosized objects is the significant influence of the surface on their properties. For mechanical properties, the surface effect is realised through the surface tension. As it is known, in nanosized specimens, the level of stresses created by surface tension may reach significant values even without loading [8]. Surface tension forces induce tensile stresses in the surface layer of the crystal, which are balanced by compressive stresses in the bulk. It gives rise to *inhomogeneous* local stress distribution within interior of the nanosized specimen. **Figure 4** presents the cross-sectional distribution of local shear stresses ξ_{ns}, which act in shear systems, where instability of crystal is observed. According to these data, even in the case of the unloaded nanowire, the value of shear stresses in a surface layer of Mo nanowire may reach values of the order of 4 GPa. This is only 3 times less than theoretical shear stress for Mo. At loading of such specimen, these stresses cause the lattice instability in sub-surface layer (**Figure 4d**). Surface tension not only gives rise to localization of the instability region in surface layer, but it is also the reason for size effect, which manifests itself in growth or decrease in strength of nanosized crystals (**Figure 5**). Recently, two approaches exist to explain

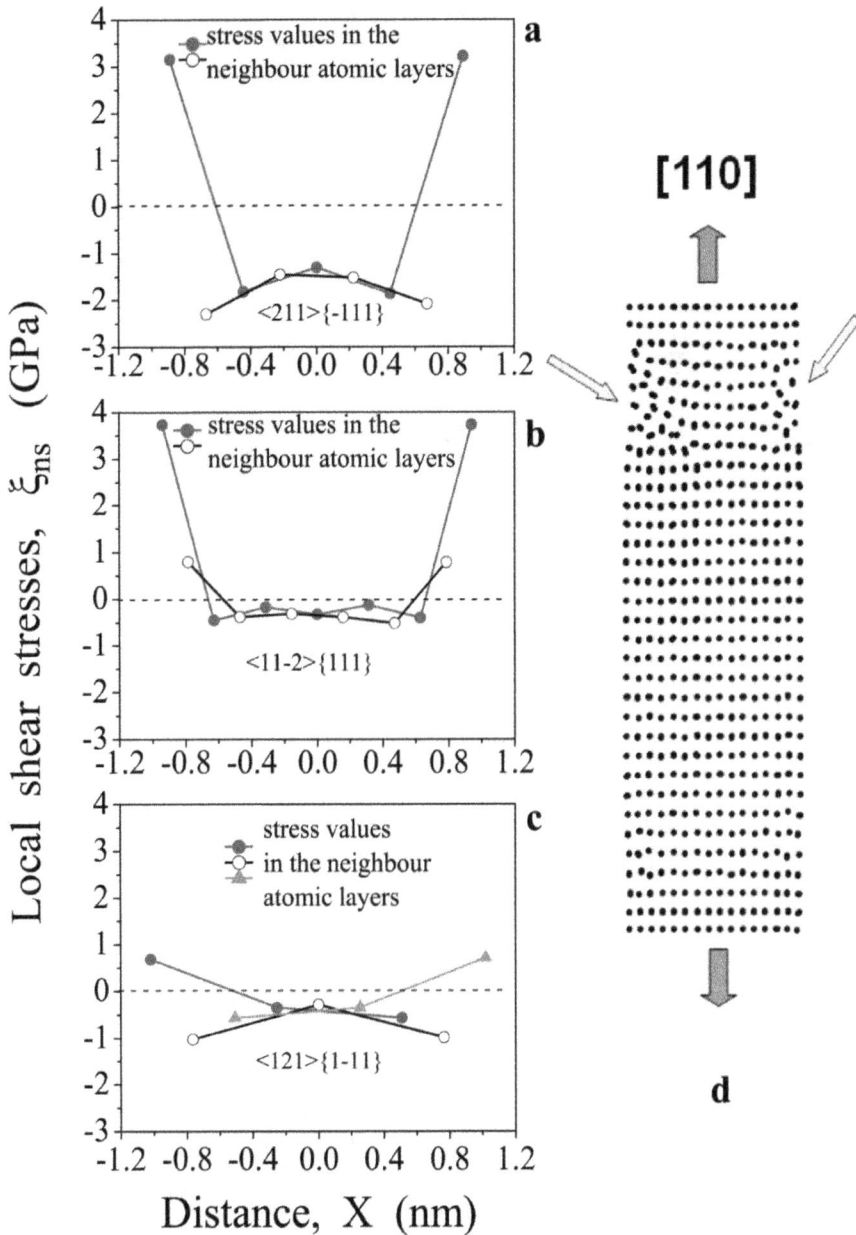

Figure 4. Distribution of the local shear stresses ξ_{ns} in the slip systems <211>{−111}, <11-2>{111} and <121>{1-11} for unloaded Mo nanowires in directions [100] - (a), [110] - (b), and [111] - (c) at $T = 0$ K. The cross-section diameter is 2.1 nm; (d) localisation of lattice instability in surface layers.

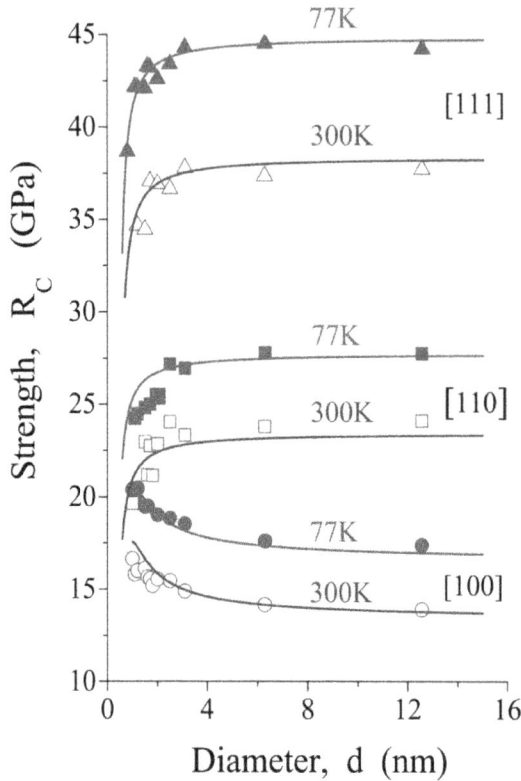

Figure 5. Dependence of strength of Mo nanowire on its diameter at $T = 77$K and $T = 300$ K for three crystallographic orientations: points are the results of MD simulation; solid lines are calculations by (12) for the following orientations (with corresponding values of parameters):[110] ($f_{xx} = 1.777$ n/m, $h = 0.29$ nm, $m = 0.470$, $\tau_c = 15.9$ GPa ($T = 77$ K), $\tau_c = 13.9$ GPa ($T = 300$ K), $\alpha = 1$);[111] ($f_{xx} = 2.345$ n/m, $h = 0.40$ nm, $m = 0.314$, $\tau_c = 15.9$ GPa ($T = 77$ K), $\tau_c = 13.9$ GPa ($T = 300$ K), $\alpha = 1$);[100] ($f_{xx} = 2.070$ n/m, $h = 0.10$ nm, $h^* = 0.40$ nm, $m = 0.47$, $\tau_c = 9.7$ GPa ($T = 77$ K), $\tau_c = 8.3$ GPa ($T = 300$ K), $\alpha = 1$).

size effect. The first of them is based on a "global" criterion of limit state [8, 10, 16], and the second one employs the "local" criterion of nanocrystal instability [14, 15, 18, 19].

Because of the surface tension, an inner part of a nanosized crystal is compressed, and the thin surface region is stretched. If thickness of this stretched layer is neglected, then compressive stresses σ_{xx}^{in} in the inner part of specimen may be estimated as:

$$\sigma_{xx}^{in} = -\frac{4f_{xx}}{d} \tag{10}$$

where f_{xx} is the surface tension along the specimen axis, and d is the diameter of specimen.

Global approach supposes that at compression of a nanosized specimen, stress σ_{xx}^{in} is "added" to applied stress, which gives rise to decrease in the global stress required for transition from elastic to plastic strains, i.e., to decrease its strength. According to (10), the value of σ_{xx}^{in} should increase with reduction of a specimen diameter. At tension, the effect of a specimen diameter on the strength must be inverse, i.e., the value of R_C must increase with the diameter growth. This agrees with findings of MD simulation of tension and compression of nanowires with fcc lattice [7–10, 36]. According to the MD simulation finding on tension of nanowires made of fcc metals (Cu, Ni, Au, Ag), at a cross-sectional dimension less than 4.0 nm, there is an increase by 10–20% of their strength level with a decrease in the cross-sectional dimension. It should be emphasised that this effect is observed for orientations [100], [110], and [111] in fcc nanowires and in nanowires of bcc metals at orientations [100] [7–10, 12, 16, 36, 37]. At the same time, it was shown in [37] that an opposite effect is observed under tension in the [110] direction of Mo nanowires. In this case, the strength of nanowire decreases with decreasing its diameter. A similar effect was ascertained for Fe nanowires [17]. MD simulation of the Mo nanowire carried out in this paper shows that for Mo, analogous regularities are also observed for [111] orientation (**Figure 5**). This difference in the behaviour of fcc and bcc nanowires cannot be explained within the framework of existing global approach. Based on the results of MD simulation and direct experimental data, it was shown in [4, 14] that under uniaxial tension, the failure of metal nanowires is governed by shear instability, the result of which is the formation of non-equilibrium dislocations or twins in the surface layer. Such a mechanism of failure is observed even in bcc nanowires at low temperatures. Therefore, in the proposed local approach, the instability criterion can be written in terms of *local* shear stresses ξ_{ns}, as:

$$\xi_{ns} \geq \tau_c \tag{11}$$

where τ_c is the critical stress of local instability of crystal in a surface layer.

To derive the criterion of nanocrystals instability within the framework of continuum approach, the concept of "effective" thickness h of surface layer can be used. This is the thickness of a layer where the distribution of effective shear stresses ξ_{ns}^{sf} is homogeneous, but their effect on strength is the same as in the case of real inhomogeneous stress distribution. In this case:

$$\xi_{ns}^{sf} = m\sigma_{xx}^{sf} = \frac{mf_{xx}d}{\alpha h(d-h)} \tag{12}$$

where d is the diameter of specimen; m is the orientation factor for system where shear instability occurs; α is the coefficient taking into account biaxial stress state on the nanospecimen surface ($\alpha \geq 1$); and σ_{xx}^{sf} is the effective tensile stress, which acts in the subsurface layer. Therefore, the value of effective compressive stress σ_{xx}^{in} acting in internal volume of specimen is:

$$\sigma_{xx}^{in} = -\frac{4f_{xx}d}{(d-2h)^2} \tag{13}$$

Using the criterion (10) with (11) gives the first approximation for strength R_C:

$$R_C \approx \frac{\tau_c}{m} - \frac{f_{xx}d}{\alpha h(d-h)} \tag{14}$$

According to this dependence, at $d \gg h$, the surface tension must give rise to decrease in strength R_C, but the degree of this decrease does not depend on specimen diameter. At small values of d (in our case at $d \leq 4 \div 5$ nm), reduction of d must result in growth of ξ_{ns}^{sf}, and, respectively, decrease in R_C. This agrees well with the results of MD simulation of tension in directions [110] and [111] (**Figure 5**). At tension in these crystallographic directions, local instability results in formation of non-equilibrium dislocation. Layer width, necessary to form this dislocation, is of the order of the Burgers vector. This is comparable with the width of stretched sub-surface layer of nanospecimen, and so, surface tension facilitates its formation. At tension of bcc nanosized crystals in the direction [100], the local instability is due to formation of non-equilibrium twin [16]. To form this kind of defect, the greater crystal volume is needed; so, the region of the crystal, where twin forms, is located in the site where the compressive stresses act. This reduces the magnitude of the resulting shear stress acting at the time of defect formation. As a result of this, the level of applied stresses necessary for the instability of a nanospecimen, i.e., its strength, increases. In this case, the upper estimate for the nanowire strength is:

$$R_C \approx \frac{\tau_c}{m} - \frac{f_{xx}d}{\alpha h(1+\beta)(d-h)} + \frac{4\beta f_{xx}d}{\alpha(1+\beta)(d-2h)^2} \tag{15}$$

$$\text{where } \beta \approx \frac{h^*}{h}\left[1 - \frac{h+h^*}{d-h}\right] \tag{16}$$

h^* is the thickness of the layer within which the defect is affected by oppositely directed shear stresses; β characterises the ratio of the slip plane areas located within the regions of compressive and tensile stresses.

The third term in this dependence accounts for the effect of decrease in total value of shear stresses influencing the twin, which is due to the fact that part of twin is located in a compressed region. As it is exhibited in **Figure 5**, dependence (15) enables to describe the effect of increase in strength at tension in the direction [100]. Thus, this rather simple model enables to explain not only the anomaly of the size effect at tension of nanowires of bcc metals in the <100> directions but also the difference between the regularities of size effect in fcc and bcc metals. For all three orientations <100>, <110>, and <111>, local instability in fcc metals is due to formation of a non-equilibrium stacking fault, the critical size of which exceeds a thickness of a tensile surface layer. As a result, for these three crystallographic orientations, the effect of increase in R_C at decrease in a specimen diameter is observed. In bcc metals, the same effect is observed only at tension in directions <100>, when twin forms. At tension in directions <110> and <111>, the inverse effect is observed, because local instability results in formation of non-equilibrium dislocations. Therefore, differences in regularities of manifestation of size effect in bcc and fcc metals are due to different kinds of defects, which form as a result of local instability of a crystal. Thus, dependence of the magnitude of the local shear stresses in the surface layer of nanowire on its diameter is the reason for the existence of a size effect for the strength of nanowires. The "sign" of this effect (increase or decrease in strength with decreasing diameter) is determined by the kind of non-equilibrium defect, which is formed as a result of local instability of the nanocrystal. When a non-equilibrium twin (bcc nanowire: orientation <100>) or a stacking fault (fcc nanowires: orientations <100>, <110>, and < 111>) is formed, the strength of the nanowire increases with decreasing its diameter. Formation of a non-equilibrium dislocation (bcc nanowires: orientations <110> and < 111>) gives rise to the opposite effect—a reduction in strength with a reduction in the diameter of the nanowire.

3.2. The temperature effect

As noted above, there are two main reasons for localisation of the lattice instability in nanocrystals, namely: (i) the effect of surface tension and (ii) the local stress fluctuation due to oscillations of atoms in the lattice. Statistical distribution of local shear stresses in nanosized crystal of iron at two temperatures is exhibited on **Figure 6**. Limit state of a nanosized crystal is reached when the local shear stresses ξ_{ns} attain the critical stress of local instability τ_c. In general case, τ_c is the critical stress, at reaching of which the highly non-equilibrium disloca-tion or twin forms in crystal. The value of a fluctuation component of local shear stresses $\delta\xi_{ns}$ depends on temperature. As shown in **Figure 6**, it leads to temperature dependence of the strength R_C.

The fluctuation component $\delta\xi_{ns}$ can be presented as:

$$\delta\xi_{ns} = t\sqrt{D_\xi(T)} \tag{17}$$

where D_ξ is the value of variance of local shear stresses in a subsurface layer, where dislocation or twin forms; t is the dimensionless characteristic of the fluctuation value. Its magnitude depends on the probability of occurrence of such fluctuation. According to the criterion of

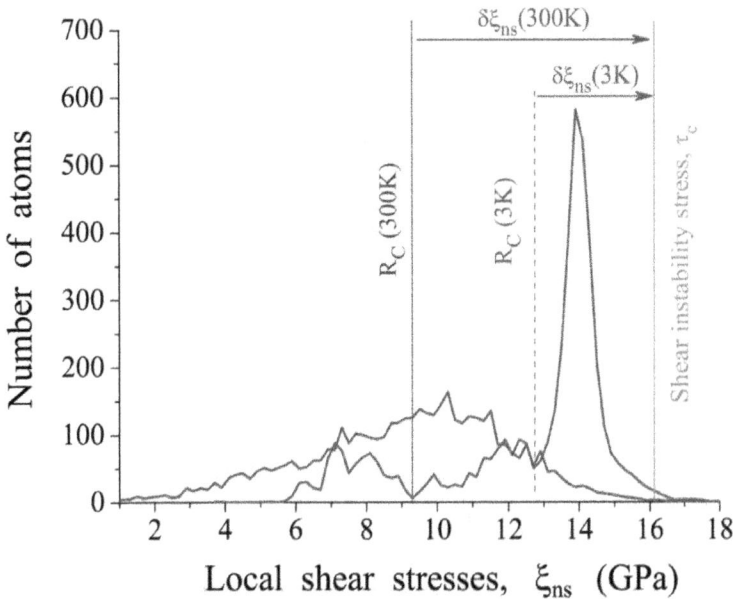

Figure 6. Distributions of local shear stresses ξ_{ns} (in the slip system ([1 $\bar{1}$ $\bar{1}$](211)) for instability point R_C in Fe–nanowire under uniaxial tension in [100] direction at $T = 3$ K and $T = 300$ K [37].

local instability (10) and expression (16), the first approximation for the temperature dependence of nanosized strength R_{un} may be presented as:

$$R_{un} \approx \frac{\left[\tau_c - \xi_{ns}^{sf} - t\sqrt{D_\xi(T)}\right]}{m} \tag{18}$$

Thus, temperature dependence of the local stress fluctuations $\delta\xi_{ns}$ (16) gives the main contribution to the temperature dependence of the strength of nanosized crystals. From the Debye model [38] and results of computer simulation [39], it follows that within the range of temperatures, greater than the Debye temperature (θ_D), the variance of atomic displacements is linear function of temperature, and for lower temperatures, susceptibility D_ξ to change in temperature decreases. In [18], experimental evidence was first obtained for the temperature dependence of Mo nanosized specimens (**Figure 7**). From these data, it follows that at temperatures higher than θ_D, the expression (18) gives the correct qualitative description of the temperature dependence of the strength of nanosized crystals, if assume the linear dependence of D_ξ on T. It should be noted that the nature of the strength temperature dependence for nanosized crystals and macrosized single crystals differs essentially because, in first case, thermal vibration of atoms

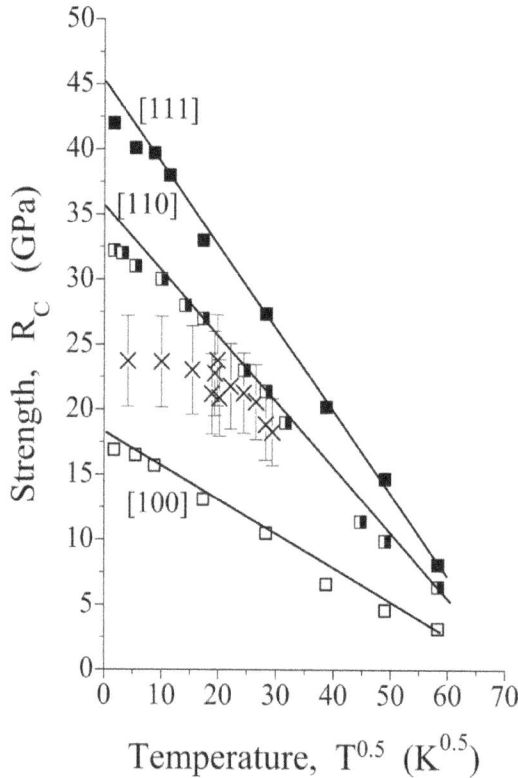

Figure 7. Dependence of strength of nanosized W crystals on the temperature and crystallographic direction: ■, ◧, □ are the results of MD-simulation, ✗ are the experimental evidence [18].

causes local instability in defect-free structure and *nucleation* of defects. In the second case, the lattice vibration facilitates *mobility* of already existent defects. It is necessary to emphasise the fundamental difference in the mechanisms and structural levels of realisation of these processes. In the first case, we are talking about the thermal activation of instability of the crystal lattice (atomic-scale event). In the second case, the oscillation of the dislocation line (a microscopic object) plays a key role, leading to the formation of kinks pairs, by means of which a thermally activated overcoming by dislocation of the potential relief occurs. As a result, the laws of temperature dependence differ as well as change in the absolute strength value. For instance, over the temperature range 77K…300K, the value of yield strength of typical bcc transition metals decreases 3–5 times, while the changes of a critical stress of NSC instability do not exceed 15–25%.

3.3. Nanosized crystal instability under hydrostatic tension

As noted above, there are two modes of crystal instability, namely shear instability and instability under the action of tensile stresses. In ideal bcc crystals, this is manifested in the existence of instability on the orthorhombic deformation path and instability on the Bain path. As mentioned above, a shear instability in nanowires is usually realised at tension in directions <110> and <111>. In the general case, when the bcc crystals are stretched in the <100> direction, *ab-initio* computation predicts the possibility of instability, both on the orthorhombic and Bain paths. As a result, the mode of instability is realised, for which a lower value of strains is required. So, for example, for an ideal niobium crystal, the value of critical strain of instability on the orthorhombic path is almost 1.5 times less than the corresponding strain on the Bain path [34]. This means that the strength of Nb nanowires at tension in the direction <100> should be governed by local shear instability. The situation with Mo, W, and Fe is more complicated. According to the results of *ab-initio* calculations, for ideal crystals of these metals, the values of critical strains and stresses on both paths are very close [33–35]. However, the results of the MD simulation on tension of nanowires of these metals indicate the realisation of local shear instability. One of the results of such instability is the reorientation of the crystal lattice from [100] to [110]. According to the *ab-initio* calculations, such a reorientation should be a consequence of the instability on the orthorhombic path. The only difference is that in an ideal crystal, this reorientation must occur simultaneously in the entire crystal, and in a nanosized specimen, this occurs locally with subsequent propagation to the entire volume of nanospecimen (**Figure 8**). These regularities were considered in the works [14, 40]. Later, similar results were obtained on nanowires with a square cross-section [16]. As a result of realisation of the shear instability mechanism at tension of Mo, W, and α-Fe nanowires in the direction [100], brittle fracture (Bain instability) does not occur, but on the contrary, the plastic strain is larger as compared with that for orientations [110] and [111] [14, 40]. In this connection, the question arises whether it is possible to realise instability on the Bain path in *nanosized* specimens made of the bcc metals. Bain instability was found in [14] at MD-simulation of hydrostatic tension of ball-shaped specimen of iron. Under hydrostatic tension, the value of the average shear stresses is zero. This contributes to the realisation of the Bain instability, since there is no driving force for the shear instability of the crystal. However, the bcc→fcc transition requires the realisation of a certain relationship between the strains of lattice along the

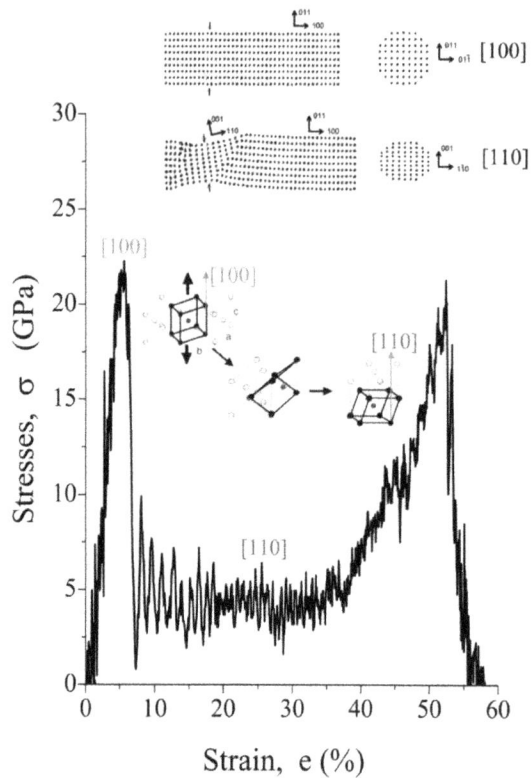

Figure 8. Stress-strain dependence for Mo nanowire. Uniaxial tension in the direction [100] at $T = 30$ K, and schemes of the lattice re-arrangement.

directions OX, OY, and OZ [34]. This is impossible to be realised under conditions of *uniform* triaxial tension. To analyse the details of this mechanism of bcc→fcc transition in nanosized crystals, hydrostatic tension of a molybdenum nanoball with a diameter of 10.8 nm was simulated [19]. MD simulations were performed for $T = 77$ K (the temperature for which the experimental data were obtained) and also for a lower temperature of 30 K. Simulation at lower temperatures makes it possible to obtain a clearer picture of atomic rearrangements, since thermal "smearing" of atom locations is reduced. Based on the results of this simulation, the diagram of deformation of the ball was built (**Figure 9**). To analyse local bcc-fcc rearrangements, for each atom, the number of neighbouring atoms in the first coordination sphere was calculated. This permits to determine the regions in crystal with both initial bcc lattice and formed unstable fcc lattice, as well as heavily deformed regions (**Figure 9**).

According to the MD-simulation findings, when critical stress of instability of a specimen under uniform triaxial tension, R_C, is reached, displacements of atoms in the specimen are essentially non-uniform (**Figure 9**). Bands form in the specimen, and deformation of the lattice in them differs from the deformation in the other part of the specimen. Detailed analysis of atomic rearrangements showed that global instability of entire specimen is initiated by bcc→fcc

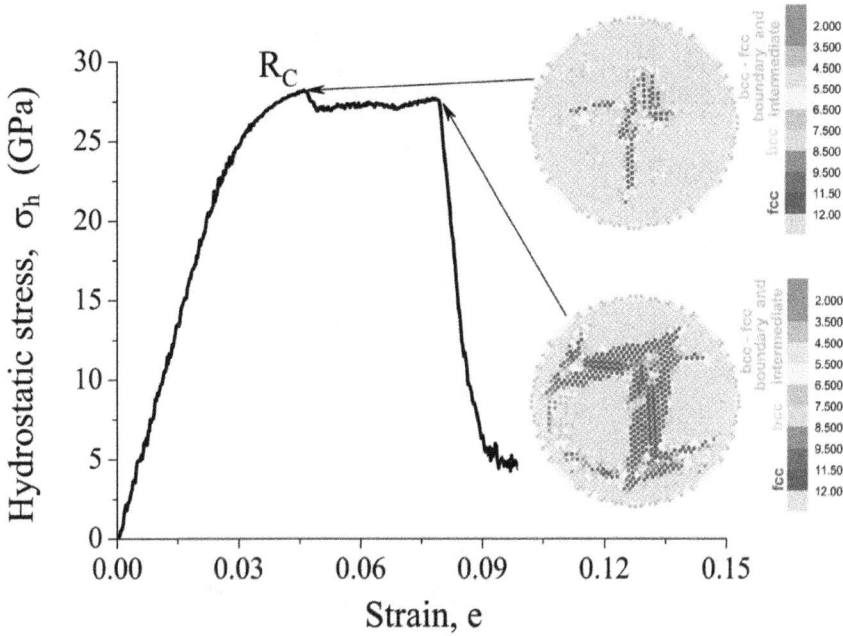

Figure 9. Diagram of deformation of the ball-shaped Mo nanosized specimen under hydrostatic tension at $T = 30$ K and crystallographic structure of the ball-shaped nanosized specimen at the moment of its instability and at the moment of crack initiation. The colour range indicates the number of atoms in the first coordination sphere for the selected atom.

transition within the local regions, i.e., instability on the Bain path is realised in these regions. At further loading of a specimen, the regions with such type of a lattice expand and new regions with fcc lattice may form as well. **Figure 9** demonstrates by different colours the atoms belonging to bcc and fcc lattices, atoms forming the boundaries between these regions, and atoms from the regions with strongly non-uniform distribution of atomic displacements (read colour).

To analyse quantitatively the instability initiation for the temperature 77K, distribution of local tensile stresses $\xi_{\{100\}}$, acting on planes {100} at the moment of instability of nanosized specimen, was built (**Figure 10**). According to these data, significant fluctuation of the local stresses $\xi_{\{100\}}$ is observed. This gives rise to change in local stresses over the wide range of values— from 10.6 GPa to 40.8 GPa at the average value of 28 GPa. The local maximum on the left branch of distribution appears due to rigid surface shell, which is necessary to realise uniform tension of specimen. According to the evidence obtained, Bain instability is initiated at the value of local stresses $\xi_{cm} \approx 40$ GPa. This stress exceeds significantly that for bcc→fcc transition at purely *uniaxial* tension $\sigma_{ct} = 28.9$ GPa [41]. Action of tensile stresses in the direction normal to that, in which Bain instability realises, is the reason for above excess. Findings of *ab-initio* calculations for iron presented in [42] show that when applying a tensile stresses in the orthogonal direction, the Bain instability stress increases as compared to purely uniaxial tension. In our case, the Bain transition occurs in one of the directions <100> as a result of *fluctuation* of *local* tensile stress in this direction. This is the feature of the atomic mechanism of

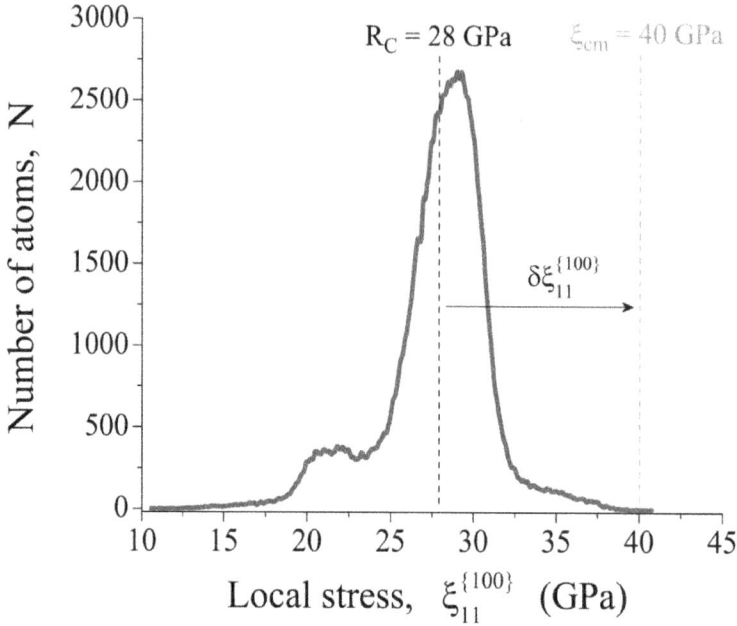

Figure 10. Distribution of local normal stresses $\xi_{11}^{\{100\}}$ in the ball-shaped nanosized specimen at the moment of it instability at $T = 77$ K: R_C is the global stress of instability of the ball-shaped nanosized specimen; ξ_{cm} is local critical stress of bcc → fcc transition; $\delta\xi_{11}^{\{100\}}$ is local stress fluctuation on {100} planes, required for realisation of the local instability of crystal.

instability initiation in nanosized specimen under global uniform triaxial tension. It should be emphasised that in this case, the appearance of fluctuations gives rise not only to excess of the local stresses over the average ones but also to deviation from uniform triaxial tension within the *local region* where the Bain transition is realised.

For quantitative estimates, the expression for value of local stress of Bain transition, ξ_{cm}, under multiaxial stress state, can be written as follows:

$$\xi_{cm} = \overline{E}e_{cm} + \nu(\xi_{YY} + \xi_{ZZ}) \tag{19}$$

where e_{cm} is the critical strain of the Bain transition under multiaxial tension; $\overline{E}$ is the secant modulus; ν is the Poisson's ratio; ξ_{YY} and ξ_{ZZ} are the local orthogonal tensile stresses.

The probability of *simultaneous* fluctuations of local stresses in three mutually orthogonal directions is many orders of magnitude less than probability of fluctuation in *only one* direction, so, in the first approximation, at the moment of local instability:

$$\xi_{YY} \approx \xi_{ZZ} \approx R_C \tag{20}$$

where R_C is the global (average) tensile stress at the moment of initiation of nanosized crystal instability.

Respectively:

$$\xi_{cm} \approx \overline{E}e_{cm} + 2vR_C \qquad (21)$$

Dependence (20) enables to estimate the value of local stress of initiation of local instability, ξ_{cm}, at a given value of global stress R_C. In this case, the experimental value of the global stress of instability of a ball-shape nanospecimen $R_C = 28 \pm 3$ GPa [19] (**Figure 11**). Assuming that e_{cm} is approximately equal to critical strain of the Bain transition at uniaxial tension ($e_{cm} \approx 0.12$ [41]); and $\overline{E} \approx 0.5E_{\{100\}}$ [19], where $E_{\{100\}} = 409$ GPa is elasticity modulus of tungsten and $v = 0.27$, one obtains $\xi_{cm} = 40.3$ GPa.

To estimate ξ_{cm}, the value of critical strain of initiation of Bain transition at pure uniaxial tension was used. According to the data of *ab-initio* calculations, the value of critical strain of the lattice instability increases at transition from uniaxial to triaxial tension, and at uniform triaxial tension, it reaches maximum value of 0.15 [42]. It means that obtained value $\xi_{cm} = 40.3$ GPa should be considered as the low estimation of critical stress of Bain transition of tungsten at multiaxial tension. In spite of this, the calculated value of ξ_{cm} agrees sufficiently with the value of ξ_{cm} obtained from the analysis of distribution of local stresses in ball-shaped specimen (**Figure 10**).

According *ab-initio* calculation findings, the instability stress of an ideal Mo crystal under uniform triaxial tension is 50.0–52.0 GPa [42]. However, such a value of strength can be reached only in an ideal crystal but not in nanosized specimens. Fluctuations in local tensile stresses are the reason for this. They do not enable the uniform triaxial tension in *local* regions of the crystal to be

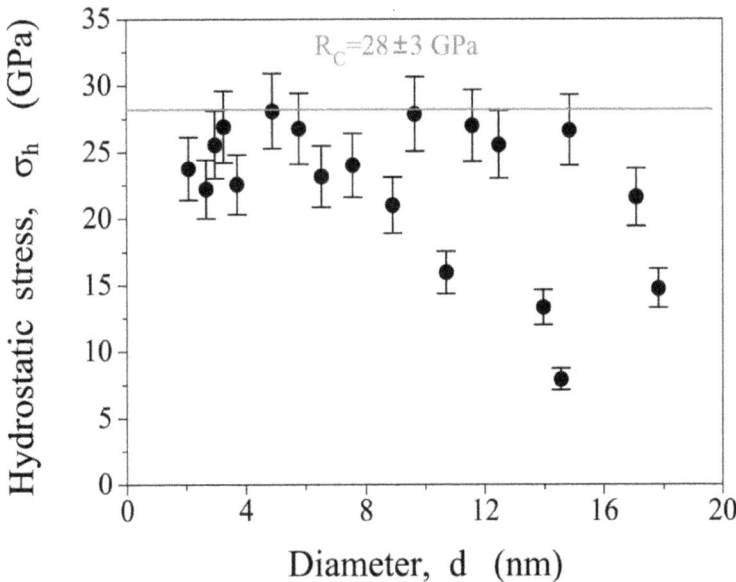

Figure 11. Hydrostatic tensile strength of tungsten nanocrystals at 77 K; d is the diameter of nanocrystal region fractured under hydrostatic tension; R_C is the experimental evidence of strength.

realised at a *global* (on average) *uniform* triaxial tension of the entire specimen. Probability of the fluctuation of local stresses in three directions simultaneously is much lower than the probability of fluctuation along one of the directions <100>; so, initiation of instability of nanosized tungsten crystal occurs at local stresses $\xi_{cm} \approx 40$ GPa. This means that in local regions, the instability occurs at non-uniform triaxial tension ($\xi_{11} \approx 40$ GPa; $\xi_{22} \approx \xi_{33} \approx 28$ GPa).

Thus, the strength of nanosized crystals under hydrostatic tension will always be below the strength of an ideal crystal under the same conditions. In this case, the strength of tungsten nanosized crystals under hydrostatic tension is 28 GPa. This is approximately 1.90 times less than the strength of an ideal tungsten crystal. The reason for this is fluctuations of local tensile stresses, which leads to: (i) exceeding of the value of local stresses over global (fluctuations themselves) and (ii) to deviation from triaxial uniform tension within *the local region* where this transition realises. For nanosized Mo specimens, the first factor results in a decrease in strength by 1.43 times, while the second one—by 1.25–1.30 times.

3.4. Strength of nanopillars and nanoneedles

Nowadays, nanoneedles and nanopillars are the most common nanosized specimens, which strength can be determined experimentally. Two main kinds of nanopillars exist, namely: (i) nanopillars obtained by focused ion beam (FIB) technology [43, 44], and (ii) nanopillars obtained by etching of nanocomposites [3]. Surface layer of specimens obtained by FIB technique contains a great number of defects in sub-surface layer, and so their strength does not exceed 1.0–1.5 GPa [43]. The second kind of specimens has no such shortcomings, and so, their strength is much higher. For instance, strength of Mo nanopillars of diameter 300–1000 nm is approximately 9 GPa. This is 6 times greater than strength of nanopillars obtained by FIB technique. However, this strength value is more than 2 times less than the evidence on MD-simulation of compression of defect-free Mo nanopillars of this crystallographic orientation [100]; according to our data, this value is ≈ 20 GPa. This difference can be caused by buckling instability, since at compression tests of nanopillars, it is quite difficult to provide the ideal conditions of uniaxial compression.

A high-field technique of tensile testing *in-situ* of nanoneedles is free of such disadvantage. In addition, it makes it possible to test the specimens of significantly smaller diameters—from 20 till 125 nm. Data presented in **Figure 12** enable to estimate experimentally strength of Mo and W nanocrystals by the value of upper scatter limit of experimental evidence on failure of nanoneedle specimens. This value for W is 23.2 GPa, and for Mo, it is 20.0 GPa. These figures also present the results of MD simulation of tension of cylindrical specimens in the direction [110]. Calculated strength values are approximately 1.4 times greater than the maximum experimental values of the nanopillars strength. At high-field treatment of the tip of nanoneedle specimen, its working volume is "cleaned" from dislocations [4, 19], and so, both decrease the values of strength of nanoneedle specimens, and their scatter may be because of stress raising related to rough lateral surface, which is formed by electrochemical polishing. The results obtained make it possible to identify the main factors leading to a decrease in the strength of nanosized crystals. According to these data, tensile strength of defect-free nanowires is always less than ideal strength. This is due to both surface tension effect (effect of a physical surface) and thermally induced local stress fluctuation (temperature effect). At transition to nanoneedles,

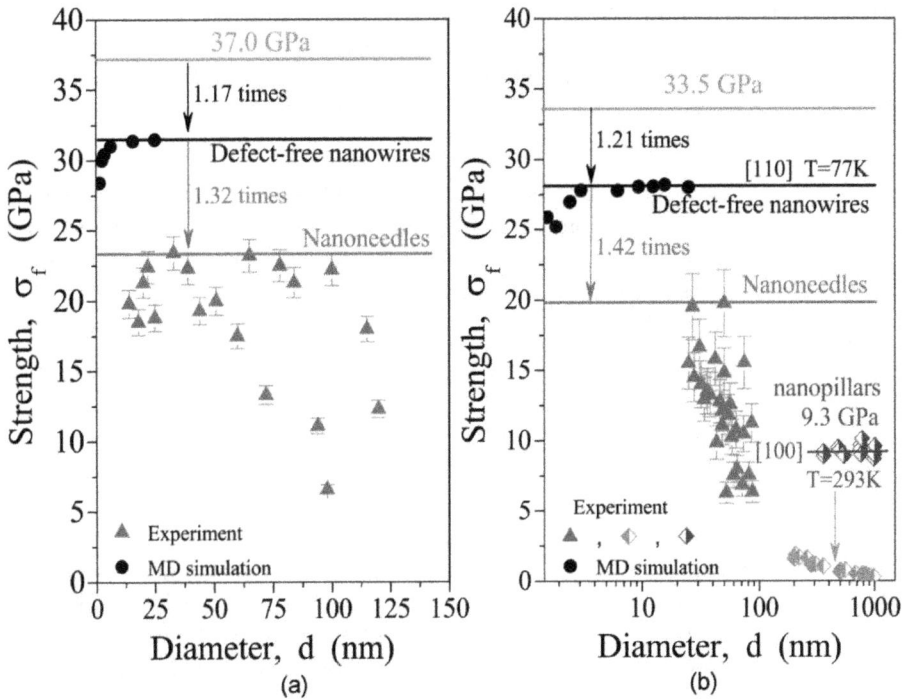

Figure 12. Size effect for nanowires, nanoneedles and nanopillars: W (a) and Mo (b); ◊ are nanopillars manufactured (prepared) by FIB technology (built by the evidence of [43]); ◊ are obtained by etching (built by the evidence of [3]).

we have additional effect of a surface roughness. This effect may give rise to a reduction in strength by at least 30–40%, and it is the cause for considerable scatter of experimental data. The strength of nanopillars is significantly influenced by the buckling effect.

4. Conclusions

1. On the atomic scale, the strength of nanosized crystals (NSC) is governed by two modes of lattice instability. This is instability with respect to the action of tensile stresses and shear instability. In nanosized crystals of fcc metals, the second mode of instability predominates. BCC metals are characterised by a competition between these two modes of instability, depending on the loading conditions of the crystal. Instability on the Bain path is realised at uniform triaxial (hydrostatic) tension. At uniaxial tension, even under cryogenic conditions, the strength of the bcc nanocrystals is controlled by shear instability (instability on the orthorhombic path).

2. Localisation of instability in a limited volume of a nanospecimen is the distinguishing feature of the mechanism of nanosized crystal instability. It occurs due to two main factors: (i) local stresses fluctuation caused by thermal vibrations of atoms and (ii) the effect of

surface tension in NSC. The first factor governs regularities of strength dependence on temperature and the feature of the bcc→fcc transition under hydrostatic tension. The second one influences the absolute value of nanocrystal strength and determines the main regularities in manifestation of the size effect in nanospecimens of bcc and fcc metals, as well as the orientation dependence of the size effect in nanospecimens of bcc metals.

3.   Dependence of the magnitude of local shear stresses in the surface layer of nanospecimen, induced by the surface tension, on its diameter (cross-sectional size) is the reason for existence of a size effect for the strength of nanospecimens. The "sign" of a size effect (increase or decrease in strength with decreasing diameter) is determined by the kind of non-equilibrium defect that is formed as a result of local instability of the nanocrystal.

4.   Strength of nanospecimen (nanowire) increases with decrease in its diameter (cross-sectional size) if the value of this strength is controlled by the formation of a stacking fault (fcc lattice, orientations <100>, <110>, <111>) or a twin (bcc lattice, <100>). Formation of non-equilibrium dislocations (bcc lattice, <110>, <111>) gives rise to an anomaly of the scale effect, i.e., to fall in strength with decreasing diameter. This is due to the fact that non-equilibrium dislocations form in a thin surface layer, where the action of surface tension gives rise to an increase in the level of local shear stresses, i.e., promotes realisation of the local instability. Size of the region required for the formation of a non-equilibrium stacking fault or twin exceeds thickness of the stretched surface layer, and this region falls within the range of compressive stresses. The latter reduces the magnitude of the resulting local shear stresses in the region where a twin or a stacking fault is formed, which leads to an increase in the strength of nanospecimen.

5.   Physical mechanisms of the thermally activated reduction in strength of nanosized and macrosized crystals are fundamentally different. In first case, the thermal vibration of atoms causes local instability in defect-free structure and *formation* of non-equilibrium defects. In the second case, the atom vibrations raise *mobility* of already existent defects. As a result, the laws of temperature dependence differ as well as change in the absolute value of strength. For instance, over the temperature range 77K…300K, the value of yield strength of typical bcc transition metals decreases 3–5 times, while the changes in a strength of nanosized crystals do not exceed 15–25%.

6.   Instability in bcc nanocrystals on the Bain path is possible under uniform triaxial tension of nanosized specimens. The peculiarity of the manifestation of "localised instability" under these conditions is that the fluctuations of local tensile stresses not only lead to a decrease in the global (average) stress required for the bcc→fcc transition but also cause deviation from triaxial uniform tension within *the local region* where this transition realises. It means that at a global uniform triaxial tension of nanospecimen, locally, bcc→fcc transition occurs under non-uniform triaxial tension. This leads to a decrease in the magnitude of stress required for such a transition. For W at T = 77 K, this decrease is 25–30%.

The maximum attainable experimental values of the strength of Mo and W nanoneedle specimens in the crystallographic direction [110] are approximately 40% less than the results of MD simulation. This may be caused by stress raising due to rough lateral surface of nanoneedle specimens forming as a result of electrochemical polishing. This means that formation of an atomically smooth surface of nanoneedles is one of the factors to reach the ultimate strength levels.

Conflict of interest

The authors declare that they have no competing interests.

Funding

This work was supported by the National Academy of Sciences of Ukraine [grants number #0117 U002131; #0117 U006351].

Author details

Sergiy Kotrechko[1]*, Olexandr Ovsijannikov[1], Igor Mikhailovskij[2] and Nataliya Stetsenko[1]

*Address all correspondence to: serkotr@gmail.com

1 G. V. Kurdyumov Institute for Metal Physics, NASU, Kyiv, Ukraine

2 National Scientific Center, Kharkov Institute for Physics and Technology, NASU, Kharkov, Ukraine

References

[1] Lowry MB, Kiener D, LeBlanc MM, Chisholm C, Florando JN, Morris JW Jr, Minor AM. Achieving the ideal strength in annealed molybdenum nanopillars. Acta Mat. 2010;58: 5160-5167. DOI: 10.1016/j.actamat. 2010.05.052

[2] Bei H, Shim S, Pharr GM, George EP. Effects of pre-strain on the compressive stress–strain response of Mo-alloy single-crystal micropillars. Acta Mat. 2008;56:4762-4770. DOI: 10.1016/j.actamat.2008.05.030

[3] Bei H, Shim S, George EP, Miller MK, Herbert EG, Pharr GM. Compressive strengths of molybdenum alloy micro-pillars prepared using a new technique. Scr Mat. 2007;57:397-400. DOI: 10.1016/j.actamat.2008.05.030

[4] Shpak AP, Kotrechko SO, Mazilova TI, Mikhailovskij IM. Inherent tensile strength of molybdenum nanocrystals. Science and Technology of Advanced Materials. 2009;10(1–9): 045004. DOI: 10.1088/1468-6996/10/4/045004

[5] Bakai AS, Shpak AP, Wanderka N, Kotrechko SO, Mazilova TI, Mikhailovskij IM. Inherent strength of zirconium-based bulk metallic glass. Journal of Non-Crystalline Solids. 2010;**356**:1310-1314. DOI: 10.1016/j.jnoncrysol.2010.03.009

[6] Mikhailovskij IM, Sadanov EV, Kotrechko S, Ksenofontov VA, Mazilova TI. Measurement of the inherent strength of carbon atomic chains. Physical Review B. 2013;**87**(1–7):045410. DOI: 10.1103/PhysRevB.87.045410

[7] Gall K, Diao J, Dunn ML. The strength of gold nanowires. Nano Letters. 2004;**4**:2431-2436. DOI: 10.1021/nl048456s

[8] Diao J, Gall K, Dunn ML, Zimmerman JA. Atomistic simulations of the yielding of gold nanowires. Acta Mat. 2006;**54**:643-653. DOI: 10.1016/j.actamat.2005.10.008

[9] Wu HA. Molecular dynamics study on mechanics of metal nanowire. Mechanics Research Communications. 2006;**33**:9-16. DOI: 10.1016/j.mechrescom.2005.05.012

[10] Yang Z, Lu Z, Zhao YP. Atomistic simulation on size-dependent yield strength and defects evolution of metal nanowires. Comp Mat Sci. 2009;**46**:142-150. DOI: 10.1016/j. commatsci.2009.02.015

[11] Diao J, Gall K, Dunn ML. Atomistic simulation of the structure and elastic properties of gold nanowires. Journal of the Mechanics and Physics of Solids. 2004;**52**:1935-1962. DOI: 10.1016/j.jmps.2004.03.009

[12] Lao J, Tam MN, Pinisetty D, Gupta N. Molecular dynamics simulation of FCC metallic nanowires: A review. Journal of Metals. 2013;**65**:175-184. DOI: 10.1007/s11837-012-0465-3

[13] Wen YH, Zhang Y, Wang Q, Zheng JC, Zhu ZZ. Orientation-dependent mechanical properties of au nanowires. Computational Materials Science. 2010;**48**:513-519. DOI: 10.1016/j.commatsci.2010.02.015

[14] Kotrechko S, Filatov O, Ovsjannikov O. Peculiarities of plastic deformation and failure of nanoparticles of b.c.c. Transition metals. Materials Science Forum. 2007;**567–568**:65-68

[15] Kotrechko S, Ovsjannikov A. Temperature dependence of the yield stress of metallic nano-size crystals. Phil Mag. 2009;**89**:3049-3058. DOI: 10.1080/14786430903179554

[16] Wang P, Chou W, Nie A, Huang Y, Yao H, et al. Molecular dynamics simulation on deformation mechanisms in body-centered cubic molybdenum nanowires. Journal of Applied Physics. 2011;**110**(1–8):093521. DOI: 10.1063/1.3660251

[17] Sainath G, Choudhary BK. Molecular dynamics simulations on size dependent tensile deformation behaviour of [110] oriented body centred cubic ironnanowires. Mat Sci Eng A. 2015;**640**:98-105. DOI: 10.1016/j.msea.2015.05.084

[18] Kotrechko S, Ovsjannikov O, Stetsenko N, Mikhailovskij I, Mazilova T, Starostenko M. Yield strength temperature dependence of tungsten nanosized crystals: Experiment and simulation. Phil Mag. 2016;**96**:473-485. DOI: 10.1080/14786435.2016.1140913

[19] Kotrechko S, Ovsjannikov O, Mazilova T, Mikhailovskij I, Sadanov E, Stetsenko N. Inherent hydrostatic tensile strength of tungsten nanocrystals. Phil. Mag. 2017;**97**:930-943. DOI: 10.1080/14786435.2017.1285500

[20] Dutta A. Compressive deformation of Fe nanopillar at high strain rate: Modalities of dislocation dynamics. Acta Mat. 2017;**125**:219-230. DOI: 10.1016/j.actamat.2016.11.062

[21] Bin MA, Qiu-hua RAO, Yue-hui HE. Effect of crystal orientation on tensile mechanical properties of single-crystal tungsten nanowire. Transactions of the Nonferrous Metals Society of China. 2014;**24**:2904-2910. DOI: 10.1016/S1003-6326(14)63425-7

[22] Rabkin E, Nam HS, Srolovitz DJ. Atomistic simulation of the deformation of gold nanopillars. Acta Mat. 2007;**55**:2085-2099. DOI: 10.1016/j.actamat.2006.10.058

[23] Zhang L, Lu C, Kiet T, Pei L, Zhao X. Effect of stress state on deformation and fracture of nanocrystalline copper: Molecular dynamics simulation. Chinese Physics B. 2014;**23**(1–8): 098102. DOI: 10.1088/1674-1056/23/9/098102

[24] Levitas VI, Chen H, Xiong L. Triaxial-stress-induced homogeneous hysteresis-free first-order phase transformations with stable intermediate phases. PRL. 2017;**118**(1–5):025701. DOI: 10.1103/PhysRevLett.118.025701

[25] Miller MK, Cerezo A, Hetherington MG, Smith GDW. Atom Probe Field Ion Microscopy. Oxford: Oxford Science Publications—Claredon Press; 1996. p. 532

[26] Müller W, Tsong TT. Field-Ion Microscopy, Principles and Applications. New York: Elsevier; 1969

[27] Mikhailovskij IM, Wanderka N, Storizhko VE, Ksenofontov VA, Mazilova TI. A new approach for explanation of specimen rupture under high electric field. Ultramicroscopy. 2009;**109**:480-485. DOI: 10.1016/j.ultramic.2008.12.003

[28] Tsong TT. Atom-Probe Field Ion Microscopy: Field Ion Emission and Surfaces and Interfaces at Atomic Resolution. Cambridge, New York: Cambridge University Press; 1990

[29] Miller MK, Forbes RG. Atom-Probe Tomography: The Local Electrode Atom Probe. New York: Springer; 2014. DOI: 10.1007/978-1-4899-7430-3

[30] Dai X, Kong Y, Li J, Liu B. Extended Finnis–Sinclair potential for bcc and fcc metals and alloys. J Phys: Condens Mat. 2006;**18**:4527-4542. DOI: 10.1088/0953-8984/18/19/008

[31] Finnis W, Sinclair JE. A simple empirical N-body potential for transition metals. Phil Mag A. 1984;**50**:45-55. DOI: 10.1080/01418618408244210

[32] Kotrechko S, Ovsjannikov A. Temperature dependence of the yield stress of metallic nanosized crystals. Phil Mag. 2009;**89**:3049-3058. DOI: 10.1080/14786430903179554

[33] Roundy D, Krenn CR, Cohen ML, Morris JW Jr. The ideal strength of tungsten. Phil Mag A. 2001;**81**:1725-1747. DOI: 10.1080/01418610108216634

[34] Weidong L, Roundy D, Cohen ML, Morris JW Jr. Ideal strength of bcc molybdenum and niobium. Physical Review B. 2002;**66**:094110. DOI: 10.1103/PhysRevB.66.094110

[35] Clatterbuck DM, Chrzan DC, Morris JW Jr. The ideal strength of iron in tension and shear. Acta Mat. 2003;**51**:2271-2283. DOI: 10.1016/S1359-6454(03)00033-8

[36] Diao J, Gall K, Dunn ML. Yield strength asymmetry in metal nanowires. Nano Letters. 2004;**4**:1863-1867. DOI: 10.1021/nl0489992

[37] Kotrechko S, Timoshevskii A, Mikhailovskij I, Mazilova T, Stetsenko N, Ovsijannikov O, Lidych V. Atomic mechanisms governing upper limit on the strength of nanosized crystals. Engineering Fracture Mechanics. 2015;**150**:184-196. DOI: 10.1016/j.engfracmech.2015.03.025

[38] Leibfried G. Gittertherie der mechanischer und thermischen eigenschaften der kristalle Handbuch der physic, Band VII Teil 2. Berlin: Springer-verlag; 1955

[39] Al-Rawi AN, Kara A, Rahman TS. Comparative study of anharmonicity: Ni.111., Cu.111., and Ag.111. Physical Review B. 2002;**66**(1–10):165439. DOI: 10.1103/PhysRevB.66.165439

[40] Kotrechko SA, Filatov AV, Ovsjannikov AV. Molecular dynamics simulation of deformation and failure of nanocrystals of bcc metals. Theoretical and Applied Fracture Mechanics. 2006;**45**:92-99. DOI: 10.1016/j.tafmec.2006.02.002

[41] Šob M, Wang LG, Vitek V. The role of higher-symmetry phases in anisotropy of theoretical tensile strength of metals and intermetallics. Phil Mag B. 1998;**78**:653-658. DOI: 10.1080/13642819808206773

[42] Černý M, Řehák P, Pokluda J. The origin of lattice instability in bcc tungsten under triaxial loading. Phil Mag. 2017;**97**:2971-2984. DOI: 10.1080/14786435.2017.1363424

[43] Kim JY, Jang DC, Greer JR. Tensile and compressive behavior of tungsten, molybdenum, tantalum and niobium at the nanoscale. Acta Mat. 2010;**58**:2355-2363. DOI: 10.1016/j.actamat.2009.12.022

[44] Kim JY, Jang DC, Greer JR. Insight into the deformation behavior of niobium single crystals under uniaxial compression and tension at the nanoscale. Scripta Materialia. 2009;**61**:300-303. DOI: 10.1016/j.scriptamat.2009.04.012

Chapter 4

Effects of Voids in Tensile Single-Crystal Cu Nanobeams

Aylin Ahadi, Per Hansson and Solveig Melin

Additional information is available at the end of the chapter

http://dx.doi.org/10.5772/intechopen.74169

Abstract

Molecular dynamic simulations of defect nanosized beams of single-crystal Cu, loaded in displacement controlled tension until rupture, have been performed. The defects are square-shaped, through-the-thickness voids of different sizes, placed centrally in the beams. Three different cross section sizes and two different crystallographic orientations are investigated. As expected, the sizes of the beam cross section and the void as well as the crystal orientation strongly influence both the elastic and the plastic behaviors of the beams. It was seen that the strain at plastic initiation increases with beam cross section size as well as with decreasing void size. It is further observed that the void deformed in different ways depending on cross section and void size. Sometimes void closure, leading to necking of the beam cross section followed by rupture occurred. In other cases, the void elongated leading to that the two ligaments above and below the void ruptured independently.

Keywords: molecular dynamics, nanobeams, single-crystal Cu, voided tensile beams

1. Introduction

Nanotechnology provides applications in an increasing number of engineering fields, with tailor manufactured products for everyday use. Mobile phones, medical sensors and solar cells are examples of well-established application areas. However, since it is an experimentally verified fact that nanosized structures respond differently on mechanical loading than macroscopic structures of the same material, design and dimensioning of nanocomponents lack a solid ground corresponding to traditional dimensioning handbook rules at the macroscale.

The reason for traditional engineering dimensioning rules becoming obsolete at small enough metric scales is that, with decreasing structural size, the number of surface close atoms as compared to number of bulk atoms increases and, at some point, no longer is negligible. Electron redistribution close to the surfaces will leave the surface close atoms in energy states deviating from those of bulk atoms. This influences the interatomic bonding forces and, thereby, the material response to mechanical loading as discussed by e.g., [1–3]. This effect is accentuated if the atoms are placed at, or close to, corners and edges of the structure, e.g., [4]. As a consequence, the material properties will vary with size for small enough structures, and the effects become obvious below about 50–100 nm.

Also, the crystallographic orientation is of uttermost importance for the material properties, e.g., [5, 6]. The crystallographic orientation imposes anisotropy in the structure and also decides the surface topology which influences the mechanical properties. The orientation further sets the preferred slip plane directions and, thereby, influences the plasticity development.

Here, the tensile response of single-crystal nanosized Cu beams, holding square-shaped, through-the-thickness voids, will be investigated with respect to elastic and plastic behavior and eventual size dependence in the mechanical response. The rational for this investigation is that even if defect-free structures might be intended at manufacturing, defects will always be present to some extent. If their presence influences the mechanical response of the structure, the product functionality might be at risk.

To this end, 3D single-crystal nanosized Cu beams of different cross section sizes, holding through-the-thickness voids of different sizes, will be investigated using the molecular dynamics free-ware large-scale atomic/molecular massively parallel simulator (LAMMPS), see [7]. The loading will be displacement controlled tension along the length direction, and two different crystallographic orientations will be considered and compared.

2. Geometry and boundary conditions

The structures considered are single-crystal face centered cubic (fcc) Cu beams of length $L = 100a_0$ and square cross section with three different side lengths $s = 6Na_0$, $N = 1, 2, 3$, with $a_0 = 3.615$ Å denoting the lattice parameter for Cu. Each beam holds a symmetrically placed, square-shaped through-the-thickness void of width w and height h, cf. **Figure 1(a)** where a centrally placed coordinate system (x, y, z) is introduced. The sensitivity to voids will be investigated by varying the width w, keeping the relative void height $h = s/3$ constant.

Two different crystallographic orientations are considered to determine its influence on the mechanical response. For the first orientation, referred to as the [100]-orientation, the coordinates (x, y, z) coincide with crystallographic directions according to: $x = [100]$, $y = [010]$ and $z = [001]$, cf. **Figure 1(b)**. For the second, referred to as the [110]-orientation, $x = [110]$, $y = [-110]$ and $z = [001]$, cf. **Figure 1(c)**.

A beam is built from the repetition of fcc Cu unit cells, and to mimic clamped end boundary conditions, all atoms within four unit cells at each end of the beam are restricted from movements in the y- and z-directions. During the relaxation step, one atom is fixed in all directions.

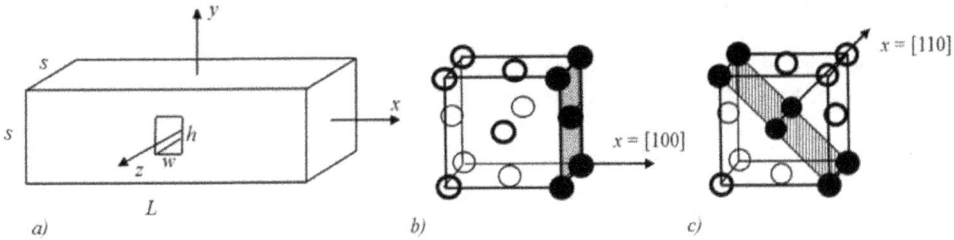

Figure 1. (a) Beam configuration and coordinate system. (b) and (c) Crystallographic orientations.

The atoms in between the clamped ends are free to move in all directions without constraints. The beams are loaded in tension along the x-axis until final rupture. The load is displacement controlled through applying a constant velocity, $v_{end,}$ in the +x- and −x-directions to all atoms within the clamped beam ends.

3. Molecular dynamic simulations

3.1. Simulation procedure

For the simulations, the molecular dynamics free-ware LAMMPS has been employed and the atomic images are produced using OVITO, developed by [8].

In the simulations, an NVT-ensemble, with constant number of particles N, constant volume V and absolute temperature T, kept at a constant temperature of 0.01 K through a Nosé-Hoover thermostat as found in [9] is employed. Before load application, relaxation of the atomic ensemble in order to reach the equilibrium state is imposed during 5000 time steps, with each time step equal to 5 fs. This gives the relaxation time equal to 25 ps, which was found to be sufficiently long to reach equilibrium with good accuracy as judged from the variations in axial stress with time. Thereafter, a constant velocity of $v_{end} = a_0/200$/ps is imposed in the +x- and −x-directions at all atoms within the clamped ends using a constant time step of 5 fs.

3.2. Interatomic potential

To calculate the atomic interactions, an embedded atom method (EAM) potential according to [10, 11] is employed. The potential has one pair-wise repulsive and one N-body attractive part and the potential energy E_i of atom i is given by:

$$E_i = f\left(\sum_{j\neq i} \rho(r^{ij})\right) + \frac{1}{2}\sum_{j\neq i} \phi(r^{ij}) \tag{1}$$

where r^{ij} is the distance between atoms i and j, ϕ is a pair-wise potential function, ρ is the contribution to the electron charge density from atom j at the location of atom i and f is an embedding function that represents the energy required to place atom i into the electron cloud. For the present study, the potential file Cu_u3.eam, provided by LAMMPS and developed by [12], is used.

3.3. Centrosymmetry parameter

The results are evaluated and illustrated using the centrosymmetry parameter, CSP, as defined by [13]. The CSP is a measure of the deviation from a perfect lattice configuration, and for an atom, the CSP is defined according to

$$CSP = \sum_{i=1}^{N/2} |\mathbf{R}_i + \mathbf{R}_{i+N/2}|^2 \tag{2}$$

Here, N is the number of nearest neighbors in the lattice surrounding the atom, equal to 12 for an fcc lattice. The vectors $\mathbf{R}_i$ and $\mathbf{R}_{i+N/2}$ are the vector pairs of opposite nearest-neighbors to the atom. For a perfect lattice, the CSP, through the definition (Eq. (2)), becomes $CSP < 3$. Since the CSP of an atom is a measure of the positions of the atoms nearest neighbor pairs, both crystallographic orientation and structure geometry are of importance. For the present crystallographic orientations and beam geometries, CSP values for atoms located at surfaces, edges and corners are shown in **Table 1**. In the present investigation, the CSP reached values up to 60 for atoms situated at or close to corners and edges. Values in the interval between 9 and 21 are found for atoms affected by local defects such as voids, partial dislocations or stacking faults.

As an illustration of the placements of atoms with $CSP > 21$, a beam with orientation [100] is shown at two different strain levels in **Figure 2**. In the figure, each individual atom is shown as a filled circle, with color according to the CSP value. In **Figure 2**, all atoms with $CSP \leq 21$ are colored red; the rest, found at edges and at corners, have their CSP in the interval $21 < CSP \leq 60$. **Figure 2(a)** shows the situation directly after relaxation, at zero axial load, with high CSP values along the edges of the beam, and **Figure 2(b)** at an axial strain of $\varepsilon_x = 0.1$, where also edges that have emerged through slip events attain high CSP values.

Lattice structure	CSP
Ideal fcc structure	$CSP < 3$
Fault sites	$3 \leq CSP < 9$
Surface atoms [100]	$9 \leq CSP < 21$
Surface atoms [110]	$9 \leq CSP < 25$
Edge and corner atoms [100]	$CSP \geq 21$
Edge and corner atoms [110]	$CSP \geq 25$

Table 1. CSP values for present geometries and orientations.

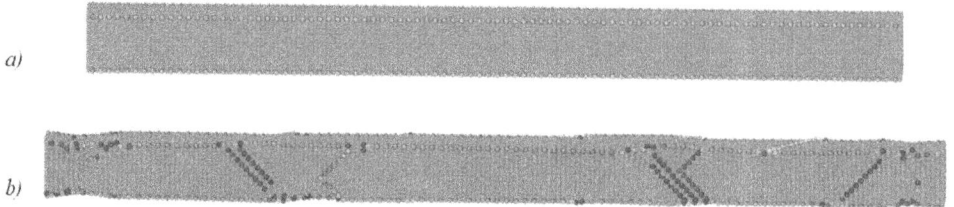

Figure 2. Red atoms: $CSP \leq 21$, nonred atoms: $21 < CSP \leq 60$. [100]-orientation and $s = 6a_0$. (a) $\varepsilon x = 0$ and (b) $\varepsilon x = 0.1$.

4. Results and discussion

4.1. Recorded strain levels

Beams of geometry according to **Figure 1**, holding voids with aspect ratios w/h = 1, 2, 3, 4, are loaded under displacement controlled tension until final rupture. After an initially elastic phase, plasticity will appear through slip along close-packed {111} planes. For each case, the strain at plastic initiation, ε_i, the strain ε_{mc} at eventual closure of the mid-section of the void, the strain at eventual total void closure, ε_c and the strain at rupture were determined through monitoring the instantaneous CSP values for all atoms during the loading process. If the beam ruptures due to necking as a result of void closure, this strain is denoted ε_{f1}. In case the void does not close, but instead expands so that the ligaments above and below the void rupture independently, these strains are denoted ε_{f1} and ε_{f2}. Recorded strains are plotted for each beam size and orientation in **Figure 3**, and the values are given in **Table 2**.

4.2. Elastic response

In **Figure 4**, all strains at plastic initiation, taken from **Table 2**, have been merged for comparison; in **Figure 4(a)**, for the [100] orientation and in **Figure 4(b)**, for the [110] orientation. From simulations of solid beams, it was observed that the strain at plastic initiation, ε_i, is, in practice, independent on cross section size for each orientation as also concluded in e.g., [14], where pure metric scaling effects were investigated for solid single-crystal Cu beams. In [14], it was found that $\varepsilon_i \approx 0.094$ for the [100] orientation and $\varepsilon_i \approx 0.068$ for the [110] orientation, so that the [110] orientation yields first, with the ratio between initiation strains about 0.7. The values for solid beams are included in **Figure 4** as circles at $w/h = 0$. As seen in **Figure 4**, ε_i tends to increase with beam cross section size as well as with decreasing ratio w/h for both orientations. It can also be noted that ε_i for the solid beams is markedly higher than for the voided beams, and in all cases, the [110] orientation initiates first.

The higher initiation strain for solid beams is expected since a void acts as a local stress raiser, weakening the structure.

Another observation is that the initiation strain for the two thicker beams, with $s = 12a_0$ and $s = 18a_0$ is relatively close in comparison with the thinnest with $s = 6a_0$, which initiates at markedly lower strains for both orientations. This indicates that a limiting value is approached with increasing s. A comparison of the initiation strains between solid beams, ε_{isolid}, and beams holding the smallest voids with $w/h = 1$ shows that, for both orientations, $\varepsilon_i/\varepsilon_{isolid} \approx 0.3$ for $s = 6a_0$ and $\varepsilon_i/\varepsilon_{isolid} \approx 0.6$ for $s = 12a_0$ and $s = 18a_0$ so that the void influence has decreased. Even so, the influence from a void, even if small, is always present.

4.3. Atomic arrangements during plastic deformation for the [100] orientation

Starting with the [100] orientation, with recorded strains in **Table 2** and plotted in **Figure 3(a)**, **(c)** and **(e)**, it is seen that for the smallest cross section, $s = 6a_0$ **Figure 3(a)**, the void closes in all cases except for $w/h = 1$. For the other ratios of w/h, still for $s = 6a_0$, the voids close first at the middle of the void at strain ε_{cm}, thus forming two separate voids. Final void closure appears shortly after, at ε_c, where after rupture occurs at ε_{f1}. The different scenarios are shown in **Figure 5**.

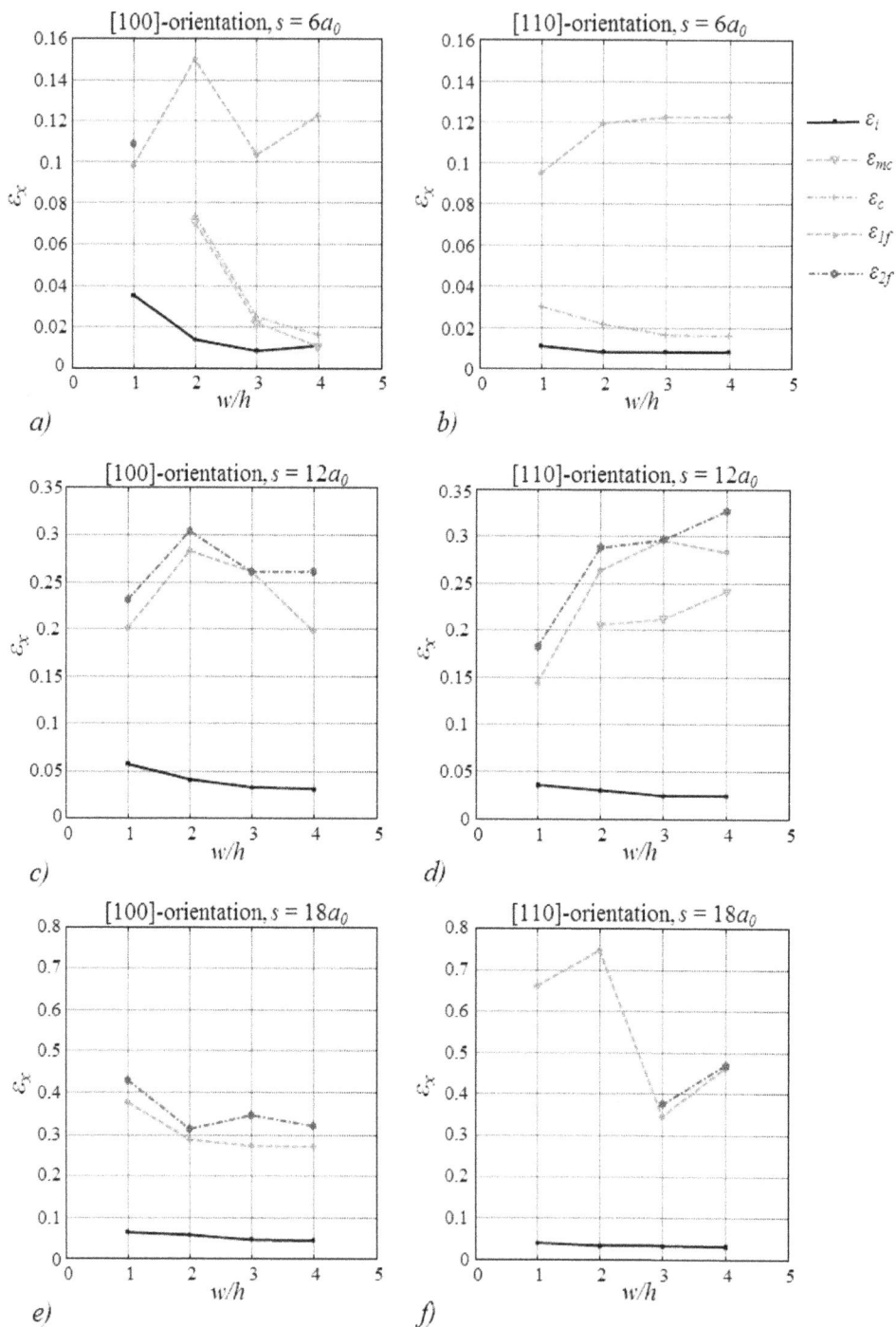

Figure 3. Strains at plastic initiation, ε_I at closure of the mid-section of the void, ε_{mc} at void closure ε_c and at ruptures ε_{f1} and ε_{f2}. (a), (c) and (e): [100] orientation. (b), (d) and (f): [110] orientation. Values from **Table 2**.

w/h, [100] $s = 6a_0$	ε_i	ε_{cm}	ε_c	ε_{f1}	ε_{f2}
1	0.0353	—	—	0.0978	0.1087
2	0.0136	0.0707	0.0734	0.1495	—
3	0.0082	0.0217	0.0245	0.1033	—
4	0.0108	0.0109	0.0162	0.1223	—
w/h, [110] $s = 6a_0$					
1	0.0109	—	0.0299	0.0951	—
2	0.0082	—	0.0217	0.1196	—
3	0.0082	—	0.0163	0.1223	—
4	0.0082	—	0.0162	0.1223	—
w/h, [100] $s = 12a_0$					
1	0.0571	—	—	0.2011	0.2310
2	0.0408	—	—	0.2826	0.3043
3	0.0326	—	—	0.2609	0.2609
4	0.0300	—	—	0.1984	0.2609
w/h, [110] $s = 12a_0$					
1	0.0353	—	—	0.1440	0.1821
2	0.0299	0.2065	—	0.2636	0.2880
3	0.0245	0.2120	—	0.2962	0.2962
4	0.0245	0.2418	—	0.2826	0.3261
w/h, [100] $s = 18a_0$					
1	0.0625	—	—	0.3777	0.4293
2	0.0571	—	—	0.2853	0.3125
3	0.0462	—	—	0.2717	0.3451
4	0.0435	—	—	0.2690	0.3206
w/h, [110] $s = 18a_0$					
1	0.0380	—	—	0.6603	—
2	0.0326	—	—	0.7470	—
3	0.0326	—	—	0.3451	0.3750
4	0.0299	—	—	0.4620	0.4701

Table 2. Strains at plastic initiation, ε_i, at closure of the mid-section of the void, ε_{mc}, at void closure ε_c and at ruptures ε_{f1} and ε_{f2}. Graphs in **Figure 3**.

In the case $s = 6a_0$ and $w/h = 1$, the void expands and the two ligaments above and below the void rupture independently at ε_{f1} and ε_{f2}. Snapshots of the events during deformation for this case are shown in **Figure 5(a)–(c)**, coded in the CSP. The state $\varepsilon_x = 0$ is taken directly after relaxation. Activated {111} slip planes are seen to appear after plastic initiation and spread along the entire beam.

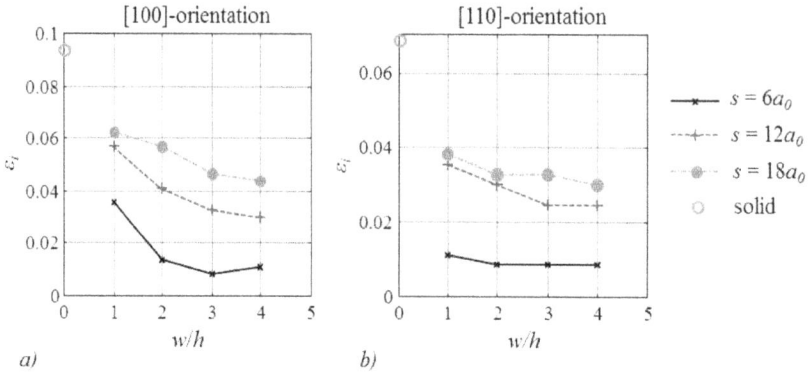

Figure 4. Strains at plastic initiation ε_i. (a) [100] orientation and (b) [110] orientation.

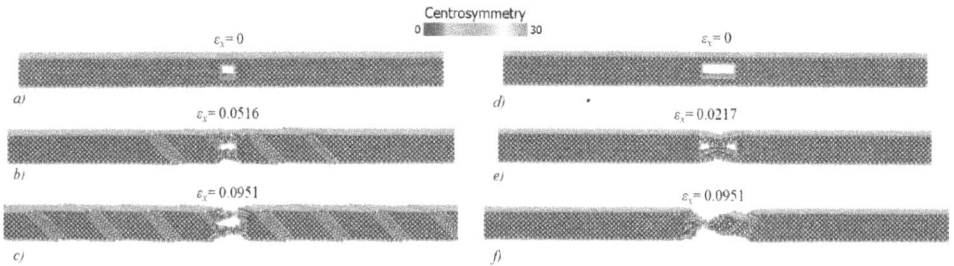

Figure 5. Events during deformation of beams with $s = 6a_0$ and (a)–(c) $w/h = 1$ and (d)–(f) $w/h = 3$. [100] orientation. Coded in the *CSP*. The states $\varepsilon_x = 0$ are taken directly after relaxation.

An example of a sequence of events during void closure is seen in **Figure 5(d)–(f)** for $s = 6a_0$ and $w/h = 3$. As seen, the void closes first at the center of the void, forming two separate voids which both close shortly after formation. This leads to that the initially voided but now healed cross-sectional part necks, and final rupture occurs at the strain ε_{f1}, cf. **Figure 3(a)**. Also, here the {111} slip planes are activated, but localization of the plasticity to the formerly voided region, followed by rupture, occurs before the plasticity has reached the beam ends. Instead, elastic regions remain away from the necking region.

For the larger beam cross sections, $s = 12a_0$ and $s = 18a_0$, no void closure occurs. Instead, the voids expand and the ligaments above and below the void rupture independently at ε_{f1} and ε_{f2}. The series of events are thus similar to what is seen in **Figure 5(a)–(c)**.

4.4. Atomic arrangements during plastic deformation for the [110] orientation

For the [110] orientation and $s = 6a_0$, **Figure 3(b)**, total closure of the voids occurs for all w/h where after the now solid center cross section ruptures at strain ε_{f1}. The voids are filled, atom plane by atom plane, from one side of the void to the other like a zipper, through slip along {111} planes. The case $s = 6a_0$, $w/h = 1$ is illustrated in **Figure 5(a)–(c)**, where the configuration directly after relaxation, at $\varepsilon_x = 0$, is included. As seen, the plasticity in this case is localized to the void vicinity, similar to the case of void closure for the [100] orientation and $s = 6a_0$ in **Figure 5(d)–(f)**.

A comparison between the corresponding relaxed states for the [100]- and the [110] orientations, at $\varepsilon_x = 0$, shows the impact of crystallographic orientation. The [110] orientation creates a more roughened surface as compared to the [100] orientation. Comparing **Figures 5(a) and 6(a)**, with the thinnest ligaments surrounding the voids and thus the weakest cross sections, it is seen that the deformation of the void in the relaxed state is much more obvious for the [110] orientation. The void seems to bulge due to the lower constraints on the atoms in combination with the orientations of the preferred {111} slip planes for the [110] orientation.

Increasing the cross section size to $s = 12a_0$, **Figure 3(d)**, displays a different deformation pattern. In all cases, the void is expanding, so that two ligaments rupture individually above and below the growing void at strains ε_{f1} and ε_{f2}. But for all cases apart from $w/h = 1$, the initial voids first close at the center, thus forming two separate voids. One of these will grow until the ligaments above and below it rupture at strains ε_{f1} and ε_{f2}. This is illustrated in **Figure 6(d)–(f)** for $w/h = 2$.

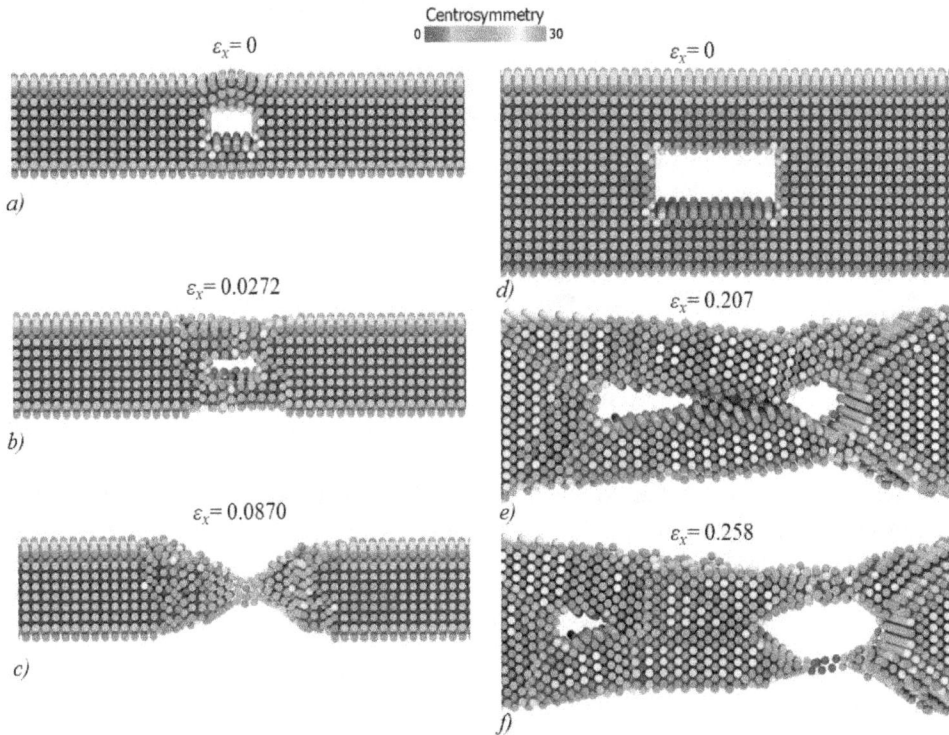

Figure 6. Events during deformation of beams with (a)–(c): $s = 6a_0$, $w/h = 1$, and (d)–(f): $s = 12a_0$, $w/h = 2$. [110] orientation. Coded in the *CSP*. The states $\varepsilon_x = 0$ are taken directly after relaxation.

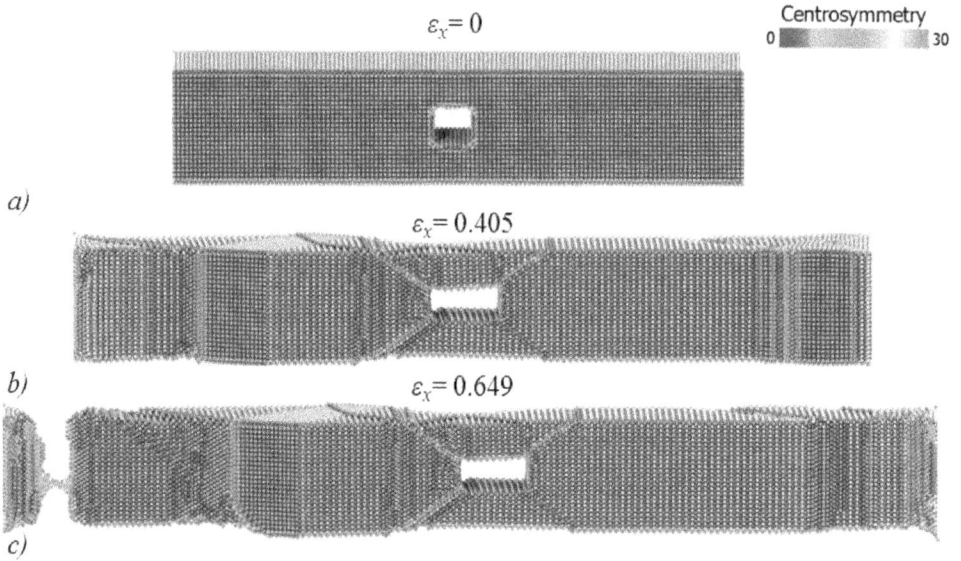

Figure 7. Events during deformation of beams with s = 18a₀ and w/h = 1. [110] orientation. Coded in the *CSP*. At (a) ε_x = 0, taken directly after relaxation, (b) ε_x = 0.405 and (c) ε_x = 0.649.

For $s = 18a_0$ in the [110] orientation with curves in **Figure 3(f)**, lastly, another phenomenon appears for $w/h = 1$ and $w/h = 2$. For these cases, initiation of plasticity as well as rupture occurs away from the void as illustrated in **Figure 7** for $s = 18a_0$ and $w/h = 1$. For the larger w/h, $w/h = 3$ and $w/h = 4$, the voids elongate and the ligaments rupture individually over the void similar to the events in **Figure 5(a)–(c)**.

5. Summary

Molecular dynamic simulations of beams of single-crystal Cu of dimensions $100a_0 \times s \times s$, $s = 6Na_0$, $N = 1, 2, 3$, and with a_0 denoting the lattice parameter of Cu, have been loaded in displacement controlled tension until rupture. Each beam holds a centrally placed, rectangular through-the-thickness defect of extension along the beam length direction equal to w and of height $h = s/3$. Aspect ratios $w/h = 1, 2, 3, 4$ were considered and the loading was applied along two crystallographic directions, the [100]- or the [110] direction, cf. **Figure 1**. The deformation development was monitored continuously and the strains at plastic initiation, at void closure and at rupture were recorded. The result is given in **Table 2** and visualized in **Figure 3**.

By studying **Figure 3** and **Table 2**, some general trends about the deformation behavior can be drawn. First in the case of total closure of the beams for $s = 6a_0$ for both crystallographic orientations, it is observed that the closure strain ε_c steadily decreases as the void width w increases. It is also observed that the strain at rupture is in the same range for both orientations for different values of s and, for both orientations, the values increase dramatically in magnitude with increasing s. Finally, it can be observed that no general trend regarding the influence of w/h on the failure strain can be drawn. In some cases, the strain increases, and in some cases, it decreases with increasing value of w/h.

It was concluded that geometrical features such as beam size and crystallographic orientation played a crucial role for the mechanical behavior. Plasticity develops through slip along closed packed {111} planes, and the [110] orientation always initiates plasticity first. Further, the strain at plastic initiation increases with beam cross section size as well as with decreasing ratio w/h for both orientations.

Studying the deformation pattern, it was found that the plasticity developed and the void deformed in different ways depending on cross section size, void aspect ratio and crystal orientation. As regards the events that lead to final rupture of the beams, different scenarios were observed.

In some cases, the void elongated and the two beam ligaments, above and below the void, eventually necked and ruptured independently. In such cases, the plasticity, through slip along {111} planes before the last ligament rupture, tended to extend away from the regions near the void and could sometimes reach the beam ends.

In the cases where closure of the voids occurred, the strain at closure decreased with increasing w/h. Also, it was observed that the strain at failure was relatively independent of crystallographic orientation and that it increased with increasing cross section size.

Sometimes the void first closes at the center, forming two separate voids. Then, two scenarios are possible. One is that the two voids both eventually close, followed by necking and rupture of the now healed cross section. In these cases, the plasticity localizes to the vicinity of the neck and leaves regions away from the neck elastic. The other possible scenario is that one of the created voids start to elongate and the ligaments above and below this void neck and rupture independently.

There were also cases where failure did not occur in the vicinity of the void; instead rupture occurred near one beam end after that the plasticity had spread over the entire beam.

Author details

Aylin Ahadi*, Per Hansson and Solveig Melin

*Address all correspondence to: aylin.ahadi@mek.lth.se

Division of Mechanics, LTH, Lund University, Lund, Sweden

References

[1] Hommel M, Kraft O. Deformation behavior of thin cupper films on deformable substrates. Acta Materialia. 2001;**49**:3935-3947. DOI: 10.1016/S1359-6454(01)00293-2

[2] Schweiger R, Dehm G, Kraft O. Cyclic deformation of polychrystalline Cu films. Philosophical Magazine. 2003;**83**:693-710. DOI: 10.1080/0141861021000056690

[3] Schweiger R, Kraft O. Size effects in the fatigue behavior in thin Ag films. Acta Materialia. 2003;**51**:195-206. DOI: 10.1016/S1359-6454(02)00391-9

[4] Melin S, Hansson P, Ahadi A. Defect sensitivity of single-crystal nano-sized Cu beams. Procedia Structural Integrity. 2016;**2**:1351-1358. DOI: 10.1016/j.prostr.2016.06.172

[5] Olsson PAT, Melin S. Atomistic studies of the elastic properties of metallic BCC nano-wires and films. In: Pyrz R, Rauhe JC, editors. IUTAM Symposium on Modelling Nano-materials and Nanosystems. Dordrecht, Netherlands: Springer Science+Buissness Media B.V; 2008

[6] Olsson PAT, Melin S, Persson C. Atomistic simulations of tensile and bending properties of single-crystal bcc iron nanobeams. Physical Review B. 2007;**76**:224112. DOI: 10.1103/PhysRevB.76.224112

[7] Sandia National Laboratories. LAMMPS. Available from: http://lammps.sandia.gov

[8] Stukowski A. Visualization and analysis of atomistic simulation data with OVITO—The open visualization tool. Modelling and Simulation in Materials Science and Engineering. 2010;**18**:015012. DOI: 10.1088/0965-0393/18/1/015012

[9] Ellad BT and Miller RE. Modeling Materials Continuum, Atomistic and Multiscale Techniques. Cambridge University Press; 2011. ISBN: 978052856980

[10] Holian BL, Ravelo R. Fracture simulations using large-scale molecular-dynamics. Physical Review B. 1995;**51**(17):11275-11288. DOI: 10.1103/PhysRevB.51.11275

[11] Holian BL, Voter AF, Wagner NJ, Ravelo RJ, Chen SP, Hoover WG, Hoover CG, Hammerberg JE, Dontjie TD. Effects of pair-wise versus many-body forces on high-stress plastic deformation. Physical Review A. 1991;**43**:2655-2661

[12] Foiles SM, Baskes MI, Daw MS. Embedded-atom-method functions for the fcc metals Cu, Ag, Au, Ni, Pd, Pt, and their alloys. Physical Review B. 1986;**33**(12):7983-7991. DOI: 10.1103/PhysRevB.33.7983

[13] Kelchner CL, Plimpton SJ, Hamilton JC. Dislocation nucleation and defect structure during surface indentation. Physical Review B. 1998;**58**:11085-11088. DOI: 10.1103/PhysRevB.58.11085

[14] Ahadi A, Hansson P, Melin S. Tensile behaviour of single-crystal nano-sized Cu beams—Geometric scaling effects. Computational Materials Science. 2017;**137**:127-133

Molecular Dynamics Simulations to Study Drug Delivery Systems

Juan M.R. Albano, Eneida de Paula and
Monica Pickholz

Additional information is available at the end of the chapter

http://dx.doi.org/10.5772/intechopen.75748

Abstract

Molecular dynamics simulation is a very powerful tool to understand biomolecular processes. In this chapter, we go over different applications of this methodology to drug delivery systems (DDS) carried out in the group. DDS—a formulation or a device that enables the introduction of a therapeutic substance in the body and improves its efficacy and safety by controlling the rate, time, and place of release of drugs—are an important component of drug development and therapeutics. Biocompatible nanoparticles are materials in the nanoscale that emerged as important players, improving efficacy of approved drugs, for example. The molecular understanding of the encapsulation process could be very helpful to guide the nanocarrier for a specific system. Here we discuss different applications of drug delivery carriers, such as liposomes, polymeric micelles, and polymersomes using atomistic and coarse grain (CG) molecular dynamics simulations.

Keywords: drug delivery systems, all atom, coarse grain, nanoparticles, nanobiomedicine

1. Introduction

Nowadays nanomedicines have a significant impact in healthcare, either for diagnosis or for therapeutic purposes, as in the case of drug delivery systems (DDS). These systems have been shown to protect the drug from external factors and/or degradation, to prolong the release rate, to target specific tissues, and to change organoleptic aspect [1–3]. The field of pharmaceutical research has developed enormously in recent years, providing new DDS for the transport and release of bioactive compounds. To achieve that, novel nanomaterials have improved, thanks to the rapid advances in material sciences, many of them with tunable properties that allow the controlled release of drugs [4]. Such nanoparticulated systems include polymeric micelles, polymer-DNA complexes, nanogels, lipid-based (liposomes, nanostructured lipid carriers) substances, and macrocyclic carriers (cyclodextrins, calixarenes), among others. DDS provide an extraordinary opportunity for the safe and efficient release of drugs, genes, and a great variety of molecules. The incorporation of nanomaterials confers physical advantages such as improved drug solubility, decreased degradation or clearance rates, decreased systemic toxicity, and improved clinical efficacy to the nanoformulations [5]. Furthermore, the sustained release of the drugs allows one to reduce the frequency of drug administration or even the dose. Finally, the process time for approval of a novel DDS that carries a drug already sanctioned by the regulatory agents is shorter, making the development process less expensive.

Relevant information on the system can be obtained using computer simulations at very different lengths and time scales: moving from continuous to the atomistic level. In this context, knowledge of the mechanism of drug encapsulation and release at the atomic/molecular level can help in the design of nanomedicines, according to the desired objective and for each specific case.

In this sense, techniques that access the molecular level, such as molecular dynamics (MD) and Monte Carlo simulations, are very powerful tools to understand biomolecular processes [6, 7]. In particular, classical MD simulations could help in the development/improvement of drug delivery systems. But, at the current computer capacity, not all nanoparticles can be studied by MD, at their full length. How to approach to this problem? For instance, liposomes are widely used DDS, consisting of spherical lipid-based vesicles whose diameters range from 30 nm to several micrometers. To simulate this kind of DDS carrier there are two possible approaches, depending on the question to answer: (i) considering a big liposome, that is, having an infinite radius, one can use planar bilayers or also simulate just a section of the vesicle, within periodic boundary conditions and (ii) on the other hand, a small liposome can be fully treated. This is exemplified in **Figure 1**. Broadly, we can access atomic details of drug-bilayer interaction using atomic level MD, but liposomes are better signified using coarse grain (CG) models.

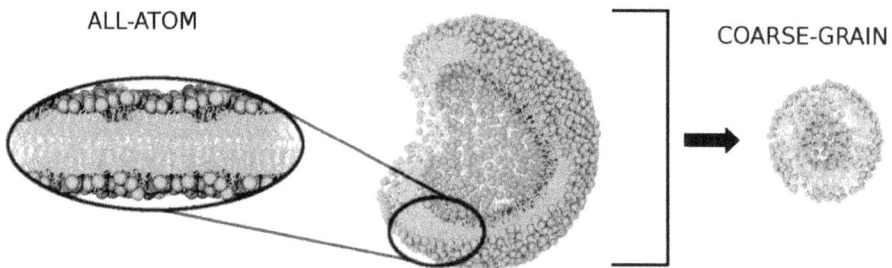

Figure 1. Schematic representation of the section of the vesicle bilayer and small liposome used as model for atomistic and coarse grain simulations.

In the following sections we will discuss fundamentals of the MD simulations and examples of simulations of drug delivery systems at the atomistic and CG level. A brief description of some approaches to study the release of drugs is also included. We finish the chapter with, in our opinion, important open questions in the field.

2. Methodology

The molecular dynamics technique has a long history [8] and it nowadays constitutes a very important theoretical tool in physics, chemistry, biology, and related disciplines. Thanks to the growing development of computing power, the MD technique is renewed continuously, allowing one to study larger and more complex systems and problems [8].

2.1. Classical mechanics approach

The physical properties of matter are associated with its structure and the movement of its basic constituents, nuclei and electrons. In principle, the evolution of a system of particles—a many-body problem—can be obtained by solving the Schrödinger equation dependent on time, which gives the probability of finding the particles in any position of space in a given time. In many cases, it is possible to decouple the wave function of the electrons from the wave function of the nuclei, following the Born-Oppenheimer approach (due to mass difference). However, even considering this approach, it is impossible, in practice, to solve the Schrödinger equation numerically and further approaches must be used (Hartree Fock, density functional theory, etc.). In particular, for biological systems (where thousands of nuclei and electrons), its resolution is impossible even under such approximations.

In this direction, molecular dynamics simulation could help to study problems of many bodies at the atomistic level, based on classical mechanics. Within this approach, Newton's equations are solved numerically. The main advantage is the realistic simulation of materials through the simplification by potentials with analytical form.

Although it is quantum mechanics, instead of classical mechanics, which describes the fundamental physics of condensed matter, the validity of the classical approximation can be evaluated based on the Broglie thermal wavelength defined by

$$\Lambda = \left(\frac{2\pi\hbar^2}{mk_b T}\right)^{1/2} \tag{1}$$

where h is the Plank constant, m the atomic mass, k_b the Boltzmann constant, and T the temperature. The classic approach is valid for $\Lambda < <a$, being the separation of the nearest neighbor. Under this condition, the entire system can be treated as a diluted gas model based on the formulation of classical kinetic theory [9]. In this case, each atom can be considered as a particle. Many biomolecular processes can be addressed by semi-empirical parameterizations that describe the interactions of pairs between the particles of the system with classic effective

potentials. In addition to having a lower computational cost, the classic models offer an adequate description of the processes and interactions. Chemical reactions (formation and breaking of bonds) and vibrations of bonds and angles with very high frequencies are excluded from the classical treatment.

Through MD simulations, information of positions and velocities of each particle is obtained, from which macroscopic observables could be calculated, such as pressure and energy.

2.2. Statistical mechanics: averages in a simulation

Here, we would like to discuss the relationship between observed properties of a large system and their microscopic dynamics or fluctuations. The particles of interest (atoms, molecules, or electrons and nuclei…) obey certain microscopic laws with specific interparticle interactions. The task of solving the equation of motion for a many-body system is still complicated and difficult, even with nowadays computer power.

Experiments are usually done on a macroscopic sample, containing a number extremely large of atoms or molecules in a huge number of conformations. In statistical mechanics, the average of the observable A over a given ensemble is calculated on a large number of replicas of the system to obtain the observables of the experiment.

On the other hand, the microscopic state of a system is defined by the positions and velocities of the particles, which are the coordinates of a 6 N multidimensional space (where N is the number of particles). The experimental observables are the averages of the ensemble and not the temporal averages. However, in MD simulation, thousands of atoms/beads are used as a way of sampling of a mechanical-statistical ensemble. How to solve this difference between the temporal averages and ensemble averages? The answer leads us to one of the fundamental axioms of statistical mechanics, the ergodic hypothesis, which establishes:

$$\langle A \rangle \text{ensemble} = \langle A \rangle \text{time.} \tag{2}$$

By allowing the system to evolve indefinitely, this means that it would pass through all possible states compatible with the constraints. Even if it impossible in practice, it is important to guarantee a wide sampling of representative conformations of the phase space when MD is used.

The ensembles are characterized by constant values of thermodynamic variables that describe the state of the system. Thinking of the simulations as a computational experiment, the statistical ensemble characterizes the conditions in which an experiment is performed. For instance, NPT ensemble has constant temperature (T), pressure (P), and number of particles (N). Each particular state, defined by these parameters, has an associated state equation that characterizes the system.

In order to mimic biologically relevant model membranes, many simulations have been done considering positive surface tension (ensemble $NP_z\gamma T$). This ensemble is chosen due to the fact that experimental bilayers are able to adjust their area per lipid in order to achieve a minimum of free energy. However, it is argued that in simulations, periodic boundary conditions limit the bilayer undulations that impact the interpretation of the surface tension. In this way, full relaxation of the simulation box (NPT ensemble) is the most used for these kinds of systems [7, 10–13].

2.3. Thermostat and barostat

In a molecular dynamics simulation, integrating Newton's equations of motion provides the means to sample the physical characteristics of a given system through its evolution in the microcanonical ensemble (NVE) [14]. Nevertheless, in order to sample other ensembles, additional variables should be added, known as extended degrees of freedom. For instance, to keep a constant temperature, the additional variables are used to control the temperature through the use of a "thermostat" [15–17]. In a similar way, in order to maintain a constant pressure during the simulation, a "barostat" constructed with additional pressure-controlling variables should be added [18, 19]. In this way, the average temperature and pressure are regulated within these variables and their dynamics. Aiming to achieve such temperature and pressure regulation without disturbing the short-term, Newtonian dynamics of the particles, the extended degrees of freedom are generally designed to evolve slowly and with only weak coupling to the dynamics of the physical particles. Whereas the fastest timescales of atomic motion are in the tens of femtoseconds, the timescales for the extended degrees are typically picoseconds or longer [14].

2.4. Boundary conditions

To perform an MD simulation, it is necessary to define the "simulation box" containing different molecules, subject to the appropriate boundary conditions to the geometry of the macroscopic system. The number of particles in the simulation box is very small, compared to an experimental sample. In this context, the border effects are meaningful. In order to minimize, usually, periodic boundary conditions could be considered. In this approach, the simulation box is surrounded by identical copies in all directions, giving rise to a periodic system that tends to the thermodynamic limit. When a particle leaves the simulation box, its image enters simultaneously through the opposite face. For bilayers, this kind of conditions is necessary in order to carry out the simulations. For other systems, like liquid droplets, non-periodic boundary conditions could be used [20].

2.5. Level of description and force fields

As we already mentioned, here we will discuss two description scales within a classical approach for the systems: atomistic and coarse grain. The main difference between them is that in an atomistic scale all the atoms (even hydrogen) are represented, whereas in a coarse grain system, atoms are grouped in beads [21]. In this way, CG models allow not only the reduction of the degree of freedom but the possibility to integrate Newton equations in a higher time step, due to the elimination of high-frequency vibration modes [22]. Usually, the treatment of interactions in the simulated systems involves the introduction of an effective force field, which allows performance of large-scale calculations of relatively large membranes and nanoparticles. This set of interaction models contains all functions and values of their parameters for the simulation.

In force fields, the potential energy could be divided into two parts, the intramolecular potential energy (the bonded part) and the intermolecular potential energy (the non-bonded part). Bonded atoms usually involve the stretching, the bending, and the torsion of the bonds. The non-bonded potential energy could be modeled as Lennard-Jones interactions and electrostatic interactions. These models are also applied between atoms of the same molecule, which are more than three bonds apart. Atoms that are three bonds apart (1–4 pairs) are treated differently in each force field.

The force field parameters are fitted to experimental and quantum mechanical data to match the spectroscopic, thermodynamic and crystallographic data of the molecule or, in the case of CG force field, they could also be derived from atomistic simulations. Among the classic effective potentials available are the atomistic force fields OPLS [23], CHARMM [24], AMBER [25], GROMOS [26] and CG Martini [21], SIRAH [27], and others [28]. The choice of the force field is a crucial step, and it should be carefully chosen since it strongly affects the results of an MD, and the number of works are constantly checking the precision of them [29].

3. What we can get from simulations?

3.1. Atomistic simulations

Within the fully atomistic treatment, only few nanocarriers could be completely simulated. This is the case, for instance, for cyclodextrins [30, 31], calixarenes [32], dendrimers of low numbers [33], and so on. Nevertheless, in most cases, in order to get information of the nanoparticles, further approaches should be done:

- small models of the complete systems: small micelles, nanostructured particles [34];
- focus on single-drug interaction with specific components of the system [35];
- internal structure of the nanoparticle in the presence of the drug;
- bilayers as a model of liposomes, polymersomes, niosomes, etc. [36, 37].

Is in this last approach where we will emphasis in this section due to the amount of work present in the literature [7, 38–43] and the direct connection with experimental model bilayers. Within atomistic simulations it is possible to explore, for instance, the drug partition in the different bilayer regions and go deeper into the main interactions responsible for their localization [37]. The drug localization could be guided by specific interactions, such as hydrogen bond [36], cation-π (for aromatic molecules) [44], salt bridges [45, 46], or entropic effects (hydrophobic drugs usually partitioned in the hydrophobic core [47].

Several biophysical techniques could be used to access bilayer properties. Between them, X-ray and neutron-scattering experiments allow us to obtain the electron density profiles that give us an idea on the overall organization of a lipid bilayer. Within the simulation not only it is possible to reproduce this profile but also access each system component contribution.

The profiles are calculated dividing the simulation box in slices normal to the bilayer and conducting the time averaging of the net charge (equivalent to the total electron associated with
each atom) per given thick slabs. Other quantities like radial distribution function could be
used in order to obtain more details on specific interactions between the drug and the lipids
or to extract information about water networks and compare with the structure factor of X-ray
experiments [20].

Local anesthetics (LA), pain-relief drugs, are among the most extensive drugs studied by
simulations in their interaction with membranes. The structure and physicochemical features
of each LA agent determine its potency and toxicity. Encapsulation into DDS -such as lipo-
somes- can modulate the anesthetic effect (onset of action, duration of sensory block) and
toxicity [5]. In this direction, simulations could guide the development of DDS devoted not
only for short-term procedures (ambulatory and surgical interventions) but also for chronic
pain treatment.

Most LAs have a pKa between 7 and 9; therefore, both neutral and protonated forms are relevant at physiological pH. Most works in literature overcome this issue studying the drug at
a high and low pH, where all molecules are protonated or deprotonated, respectively. From
MD simulation, most authors report neutral LA partition in the hydrophobic region of the
bilayer and the protonated species in the lipid head/water interface and water phase, with
differences between them (depending on hydrophilicity, steric factors, the lipid bilayer, etc.)
[47–53]. For instance, the behavior described for lidocaine in 1,2-dimyristo yl-sn-glycero-
3-phosphocholine (DMPC) is similar to the one reported by us, using prilocaine in 1-Palmitoyl-
2-oleoylphosphatidylcholine (POPC), even using different force fields (GROMOS and
CHARMM27, respectively) [48, 50]. In both cases the neutral drug presents a bimodal distribution. Also, crossing events, defined as the drug crossing from one monolayer to the other
bilayer, were observed for both drugs. On the other hand, in our knowledge, no crossing events
were reported for any protonated LA, even in long simulations (400ns, Slipid force field) [53].
The differential distribution of prilocaine (PLC) depending on its ionization state is illustrated
inside the bilayer as shown in **Figure 2A**. On the other hand, more hydrophobic LA at the neutral state, such as etidocaine, shows higher distribution than prilocaine in the bilayer core [50].
The localization of the etidocaine in this region promotes a higher disorder in the lipid chains.
This property could be accessed through the calculation of the order parameter, defined by:

$$S_{mol} = \frac{1}{2}\langle 3\cos^2\theta_n - 1\rangle \tag{3}$$

Here, θ_n is the angle between the normal to the bilayer and the normal to the plane defined by
two carbon-hydrogen bonds. The order parameter is related to the tilt angle of the chains and
to the *trans-gauche* distribution of chain dihedrals. The effects on the lipid packing from guest
molecules such as PLC distributed within membranes can be experimentally determined
from changes in the carbon-deuterium segmental order parameter along the lipid chain.
In that case, the experimental order parameter, $S_{CD} = -1/2S_{mol}$, is derived from the measured
quadrupole splitting $\Delta v = (3/4)(e^2qQ/h)S_{CD}$ [54, 55]. In **Figure 2B** we show the order parameter
of POPC neat and containing etidocaine.

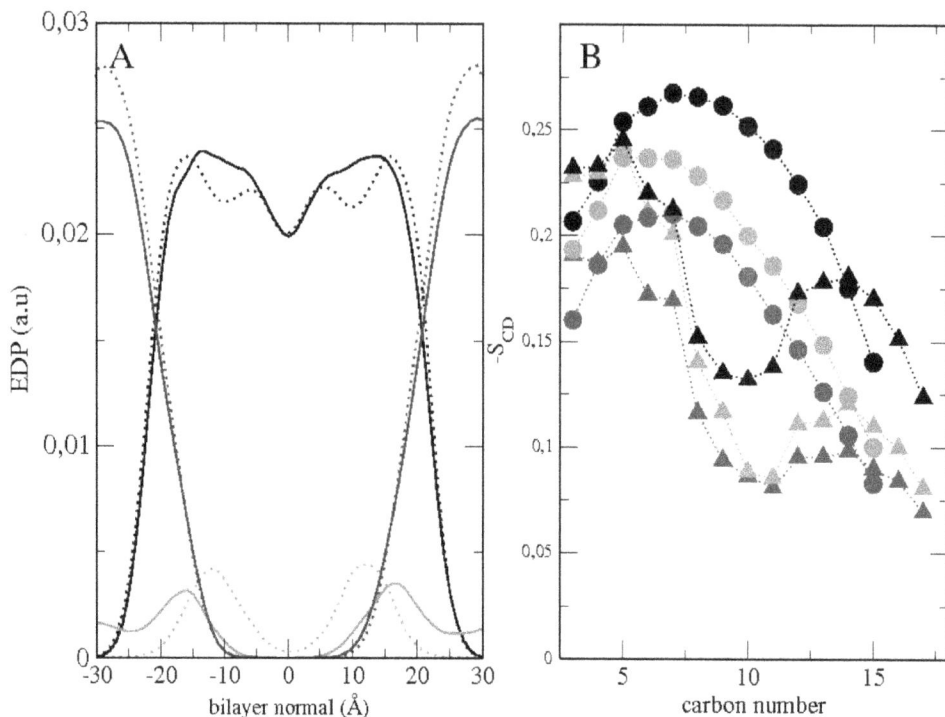

Figure 2. (A) Electron density profiles (EDPs) of different bilayer components as a function of the membrane normal: POPC in black, water in blue and drug in red. Solid and dotted line are used for protonated and neutral prilocaine, respectively. (B) Calculated order parameter, $-SCD$, for plain bilayers (black); etidocaine at 1:6 and 1:3 drug:lipid ratio in green and violet, respectively. Circles and circles are used for saturated and unsaturated chains of POPC.

In a similar direction, simulations with the two bupivacaine (BVC) enantiomers helped to elucidate the higher cardiotoxicity observed for the R-form than the S-form [56]. The effect of R-BVCs (at 1:3 molar concentration) is to disorganize the membrane (decrease the order parameters); this effect is seen for both tails [51]. This is essentially related with the empty space in the lower part of the lipid tails due to the localization of the LA and the lateral expansion of the bilayer. On the other hand, S-BVC only promotes a soft disorganization for carbons above 10 (in both tails): in this case, the localization of the LA in the interior of the bilayer compensates the effects of the lateral expansion.

Thus, in our hands, molecular simulation of LA in model membranes was found useful to explain different aspects on the anesthesia mechanism and drug encapsulation [57]. Besides, within simulations, it was possible to explain the experimentally observed differences [49] between less (prilocaine/lidocaine) and more hydrophobic (etidocaine) isomers regarding the depth of their preferential insertion into bilayers [50], with possible implication on the increased potency and toxicity of the more hydrophobic analogs (Meyer-Overton rule) [5, 58].

3.2. Coarse grain

Through the reduction of degrees of freedom, CG models are useful to efficiently simulate drug delivery systems, such as liposomes, polymersome, and micelles, relieving the size and time-scale limitations of atomistic simulation but losing in details. One of the crucial factors, representing the capacity of potential drug delivery systems, is the partition coefficient of a potential drug candidate between the aggregate and surrounding water.

In particular, the encapsulation of prilocaine into liposome was studied using this approach (MARTINI-based force field) [59]. Following the atomistic results, neutral PLC was fully encapsulated in the interior part of the lipid membrane where it adopts an asymmetric bimodal distribution. Our simulation results therefore suggest that although protonation leads to a structured interaction between drug and host, hydrophobicity is the major driving force of drug encapsulation. Our results also depend on the protonated PLC initial simulations conditions [59]. This observation suggested different preparation schemes of liposome-drug complexes, leading to prilocaine trapped within vesicles that could increase overall drug encapsulation efficiency.

On the other hand, it is demonstrated that the two LA species (neutral and protonated) are present at physiologic pH, contributing together to the anesthetic effect [50, 57] and they could be important in the development of DDS. For example, in a liposomal formulation prepared at pH 7.4, while the neutral form of the anesthetic is able to quickly and efficiently cross the bilayer, the protonated form is mainly found in the water phase. Both species depend on each other: the protonated needs the neutral one in order to efficiently cross the membrane, reaching the adjacent water compartment, while the uncharged species depends on the high solubility of the protonated LA in the water phase to reach the clinically effective dose.

The protonation/deprotonation reaction cannot be directly simulated using classical MD simulation. In order to partially overcome this, we represented the physiological pH, taking into account Henderson-Hasselbach equation:

$$pH = pKa + \log \frac{[neutral\ PLC]}{[protonated\ PLC]} \qquad (4)$$

and the fact that PLC apparent pKa in membranes is 7.6 [60]; values around 0.4 and 0.6 represent the molar fractions of neutral and protonated species, respectively.

In **Figure 3A**, we illustrated the results with a snapshot. In order to get an idea of how PLCs distribute inside the vesicle, we have calculated the average number of PLCs as a function of the PLC (center of mass) distance to the vesicle center. In **Figure 3**, we also show separated histograms for neutral (B) and protonated (C) PLCs. Considering that the average vesicle radius is 75Å, we can see from **Figure 3C** that all neutral PLCs are essentially found inside the vesicle and show two main peaks, in good agreement with previous results [47, 57]. On the other hand, just a small fraction (~14 molecules on an average) of the protonated

PLCs are found inside the vesicle, as we can see in **Figure 3C**, and they only interact with the external monolayer of the vesicle. The results here show that the behavior of PLCs at physiological pH is essentially a combination of high and low pH: This means neutral PLCs are found inside the vesicle, whereas protonated molecules are partitioned into the external monolayer of the vesicle and water regions. However, different than at low pH, the average number of protonated PLCs inside the vesicle is lower at physiological pH (14 than 20) because of the presence of neutral molecules. In this direction, this kind of simulation could guide the LA:lipid molar ratio to enhance the loading capacity of the liposomes, depending on pH.

Similar to liposomes, polymersomes form a core-shell structure allowing us to encapsulate both hydrophilic and hydrophobic molecules. These synthetic polymer vesicles are composed

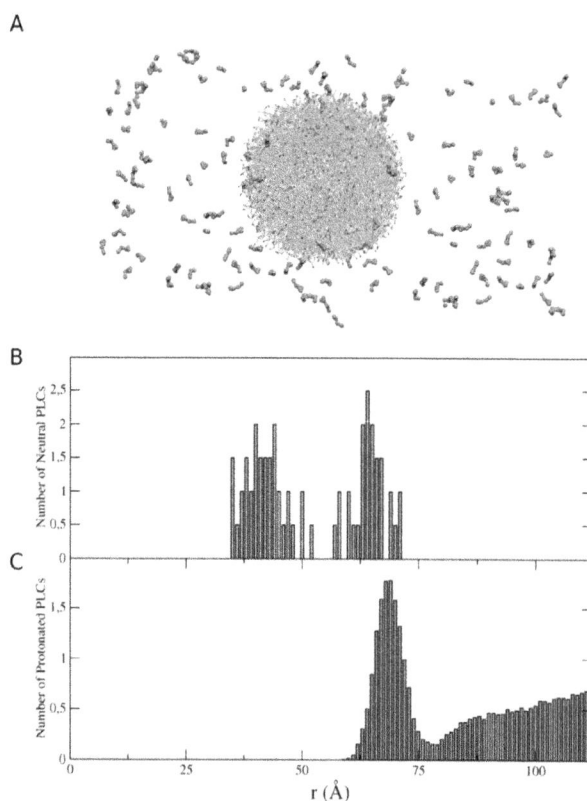

Figure 3. (A) and (B) Snapshots from the molecular dynamics simulations prilocaine in POPC vesicles at physiological pH. The snapshots correspond to the initial configuration and after 1 µs NVT simulation run. Neutral and protonated PLC molecules are shown in magenta-blue and in brown, respectively, and lipids are in blue and green forming the vesicle. Water sites were removed for visualization purposes. The chlorine counter ions, in red, are only shown in the last configuration. Number of neutral (C) and protonated (B) PLCs as function of the PLCs center of mass distance to the center of the vesicle.

of block copolymer amphiphiles that in the presence of water self-assemble in an orga-
nized structures, attracting special interest due to their tunable properties for drug delivery.
However, since polymersome sizes often range from 100 nm up to the micron diameter size
it is difficult to simulate, even at the coarse grain level, a big polymersome. In this direction,
the simulation of polymeric bilayers and small polymersomes at a CG level would make possible to study key mechanical and structural properties to better develop these kinds of drug
delivery systems, as recently explored by us [12]. Moreover, these simulations are useful to
shed light into the effects of the incorporation of model drugs (such as neutral and protonated
prilocaine), as we explore in a work-in-progress study.

Other popular drug delivery systems composed of copolymers are micelles. Several examples
are found in literature [61–66]. In this regard, the encapsulation of the hydrophilic antimi-
graine drug sumatriptan in a polymer micelle was studied by us in a recent work [13]. A
micelle composed of the pluronic F127 tri-block copolymer was simulated under different
initial conditions. The main results showed that the drug essentially partitioned in the hydrophilic drug with little effect in the overall micellar structure, and size also correlated with
experimental studies.

3.3. Drug release: free energy calculations

The times required to observe the mechanism of drug release are out of reach using MD
simulations. Nevertheless, important information could be obtained by calculating, for
instance, the free energy through a given path for the drug leaving the nanostructure. The
idea of enhancement of the sampling of configurational space is not new in molecular simulations, and several methods such as umbrella sampling [67, 68], adaptive biasing force
(ABF) method [69], the Wang-Landau algorithm [70], steer molecular dynamics [71], and
metadynamics have been proposed [53]. In order to investigate the release of the drug using
these methods, a reaction path should be chosen. For bilayers, the natural path is the z direction (normal to the bilayer) and for spherical nanoparticles the radius of it, as exemplified
in **Figure 4A** and **B**, respectively.

For the case of local anesthetics, very recently, Saaedi et al. estimated the free energy profile
of lidocaine and articaine in a DMPC lipid bilayer using well-tempered metadynamics simulations (Slipid force field) [53]. They estimated that the free energy between the well and the
water phase was −32.9kj/mol and −25.4 kj/mol for neutral lidocaine and articaine, respectively.
On the other hand, this value reduces ~20% for the protonated species. Similar results were
obtained by Prates et al. (unpublished results) using ABF, who reported a free energy difference ~24kj/mol in a POPC membrane using the NP_zAT ensemble. This means that pH is a
determinant factor for the encapsulation/release of these drugs.

These calculations could be also carried out using a CG approach. Nevertheless, qualitative
information could come across of these kinds of calculations. For example, Loverde et al. used
Steered molecular dynamics to estimate the free energy profile of Taxol (an anticancer drug)
when pulled out from a micelle core [72].

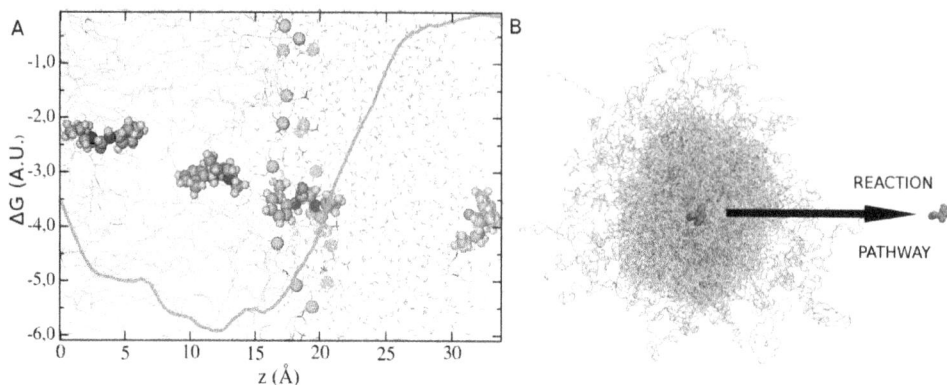

Figure 4. Schematic representations (A) a free energy profile over the lipid bilayer normal and (B) a micelle, as generic DDS, showing the reaction pathway.

4. Final remarks and challenges

The rapid development of the field due to the entanglement between computer capabilities and algorithm development, open the possibility to imagine many applications of the MD approach in drug delivery systems. Till now, we have explored different applications on the molecular dynamics techniques to study drug delivery systems based on the available literature.

We would like to mention what we consider to be the next desirable steps in the field:

- In our knowledge, most of free energy calculations reported in the literature were simulated with a single drug, without taking into account the drug-loaded medium. In this way, important information could be obtained from these calculations.

- To obtain semi-quantitative information into the loading capacity of a specific drug into a given DDS.

- The use of a constant pH ensemble [73] could be applied to these kinds of systems. This represents a challenge in order to get on-the-fly protonation/deprotonation of molecules depending on the surrounding environment. This will emulate the loading and release of the DDS that could happen in different conditions.

- Through the calculation of the different components of the pressure tensor, it's possible to access mechanical properties that could guide the DDS development.

- New DDS systems could be addressed with this technique. One example of this is the reconstituted high-density lipoprotein particles to deliver hydrophobic drugs to impaired cells and tissues [74]. These nanostructures are being used for other things such as protein stabilization, but the possibility to develop drug delivery systems with them is a promising one that could take advantages of molecular dynamics simulations.

- New applications for old drugs, as well as new therapies like gene delivery, could benefit from this computational approach [75].

Author details

Juan M.R. Albano[1,2], Eneida de Paula[3] and Monica Pickholz[1,2*]

*Address all correspondence to: monicapickholz@gmail.com

1 Physics Institute of Buenos Aires (IFIBA, UE UBA-CONICET), Buenos Aires, Argentina

2 Physics Department of the FCEyN (University of Buenos Aires), Buenos Aires, Argentina

3 Biology Institute of the University of Campinas, Campinas, Brazil

References

[1] Tiwari G, Tiwari R, Bannerjee S, et al. Drug delivery systems: An updated review. International Journal of Pharmaceutical Investigation. 2012;2:2. DOI: 10.4103/2230-973X.96920

[2] Ulbrich K, Holá K, Šubr V, et al. Targeted drug delivery with polymers and magnetic nanoparticles: Covalent and noncovalent approaches, release control, and clinical studies. Chemical Reviews. 2016;116:5338-5431. DOI: 10.1021/acs.chemrev.5b00589

[3] Karimi M, Ghasemi A, Sahandi Zangabad P, et al. Smart micro/nanoparticles in stimulus-responsive drug/gene delivery systems. Chemical Society Reviews. 2016;45:1457-1501. DOI: 10.1039/C5CS00798D

[4] Caster JM, Patel AN, Zhang T, Wang A. Investigational nanomedicines in 2016: A review of nanotherapeutics currently undergoing clinical trials. Wiley Interdisciplinary Reviews. Nanomedicine Nanobiotechnology. 2017;9:e1416. DOI: 10.1002/wnan.1416

[5] de Paula E, Cereda CM, Fraceto LF, et al. Micro and nanosystems for delivering local anesthetics. Expert Opinion on Drug Delivery. 2012;9:1505-1524. DOI: 10.1517/17425247.2012. 738664

[6] Villalobos R, Garcia E, Quintanar D, Young P. Drug release from inert spherical matrix systems using Monte Carlo simulations. Current Drug Delivery. 2017;14:65-72. DOI: 10. 2174/1567201813666160512145800

[7] Lopes D, Jakobtorweihen S, Nunes C, et al. Shedding light on the puzzle of drug-membrane interactions: Experimental techniques and molecular dynamics simulations. Progress in Lipid Research. 2017;65:24-44. DOI: 10.1016/j.plipres.2016.12.001

[8] Gelpi J, Hospital A, Goñi R, Orozco M. Molecular dynamics simulations: Advances and applications. Advances and Applications in Bioinformatics and Chemistry. 2015;8:37-47 DOI: 10.2147/AABC.S70333

[9] Morgon NH, Coutinho KR. Métodos de química teórica e modelagem molecular. Sao Paulo, Brazil: Editora Livraria da Física; 2007

[10] Florencia Martini M, Disalvo EA, Pickholz M. Nicotinamide and picolinamide in phospholipid monolayers. International Journal of Quantum Chemistry. 2012;112:3289-3295. DOI: 10.1002/qua.24124

[11] Wood I, Martini MF, Albano JMR, et al. Coarse grained study of pluronic F127: Comparison with shorter co-polymers in its interaction with lipid bilayers and self-aggregation in water. Journal of Molecular Structure. 2016;**1109**:106-113. DOI: 10.1016/j. molstruc.2015.12.073

[12] Grillo DA, Albano JMR, Mocskos EE, et al. Diblock copolymer bilayers as model for poly-mersomes: A coarse grain approach. The Journal of Chemical Physics. 2017;**146**:244904. DOI: 10.1063/1.4986642

[13] Wood I, Albano JMR, Filho PLO, et al. A sumatriptan coarse-grained model to explore different environments: Interplay with experimental techniques. European Biophysics Journal. 2018. In press. DOI: 10.1007/s00249-018-1278-2

[14] Lippert RA, Predescu C, Ierardi DJ, et al. Accurate and efficient integration for molecular dynamics simulations at constant temperature and pressure. The Journal of Chemical Physics. 2013;**139**:164106. DOI: 10.1063/1.4825247

[15] Ryckaert J-P, Ciccotti G, Berendsen HJ. Numerical integration of the cartesian equations of motion of a system with constraints: Molecular dynamics of n-alkanes. Journal of Computational Physics. 1977;**23**:327-341. DOI: 10.1016/0021-9991(77)90098-5

[16] Feller SE, Zhang Y, Pastor RW, Brooks BR. Constant pressure molecular dynamics simu-lation: The Langevin piston method. Journal of Chemical Physics. 1995;**103**:4613-4621. DOI: 10.1063/1.470648

[17] Evans DJ, Holian BL. The Nose–Hoover thermostat. The Journal of Chemical Physics. 1985;**83**:4069-4074. DOI: 10.1063/1.449071

[18] Parrinello M, Rahman A. Polymorphic transitions in single crystals: A new molecular dynamics method. Journal of Applied Physics. 1981;**52**:7182-7190. DOI: 10.1063/1.328693

[19] Berendsen HJC, Postma JPM, van Gunsteren WF, et al. Molecular dynamics with cou-pling to an external bath. The Journal of Chemical Physics. 1984;**81**:3684-3690. DOI: 10.1063/1.448118

[20] Leach AR. Molecular Modelling: Principles and Applications. Edinburgh, UK: Prentice Hall; 2001

[21] Marrink SJ, Risselada HJ, Yefimov S, et al. The MARTINI force field: Coarse grained model for biomolecular simulations. The Journal of Physical Chemistry B. 2007;**111**:7812-7824. DOI: 10.1021/jp071097f

[22] Winger M, Trzesniak D, Baron R, van Gunsteren WF. On using a too large integra-tion time step in molecular dynamics simulations of coarse-grained molecular models. Physical Chemistry Chemical Physics. 2009. DOI: 10.1039/b818713d

[23] Jorgensen WL, Maxwell DS, Tirado-Rives J. Development and testing of the OPLS all-atom force field on conformational energetics and properties of organic liquids. Journal of the American Chemical Society. 1996;**118**:11225-11236. DOI: 10.1021/ja9621760

[24] Best RB, Zhu X, Shim J, et al. Optimization of the additive CHARMM all-atom protein force field targeting improved sampling of the backbone φ, ψ and side-chain $\chi 1$ and $\chi 2$ dihedral angles. Journal of Chemical Theory and Computation. 2012;**8**:3257-3273. DOI: 10.1021/ct300400x

[25] Wang J, Wolf RM, Caldwell JW, et al. Development and testing of a general amber force field. Journal of Computational Chemistry. 2004;**25**:1157-1174. DOI: 10.1002/jcc.20035

[26] Ott K-H, Meyer B. Parametrization of GROMOS force field for oligosaccharides and assessment of efficiency of molecular dynamics simulations. Journal of Computational Chemistry. 1996;**17**:1068-1084. DOI: 10.1002/(SICI)1096-987X(199606)17:8<1068::AID-JCC14>3.0.CO;2-A

[27] Darré L, Machado MR, Brandner AF, et al. SIRAH: A structurally unbiased coarse-grained force field for proteins with aqueous solvation and long-range electrostatics. Journal of Chemical Theory and Computation. 2015;**11**:723-739. DOI: 10.1021/ct5007746

[28] Izvekov S, Parrinello M, Burnham CJ, Voth GA. Effective force fields for condensed phase systems from ab initio molecular dynamics simulation: A new method for force-matching. The Journal of Chemical Physics. 2004;**120**:10896-10913. DOI: 10.1063/1.1739396

[29] Paloncýová M, Fabre G, DeVane RH, et al. Benchmarking of force fields for molecule–membrane interactions. Journal of Chemical Theory and Computation. 2014;**10**: 4143-4151. DOI: 10.1021/ct500419b

[30] de Jesus MB, Fraceto LF, Martini MF, et al. Non-inclusion complexes between riboflavin and cyclodextrins. The Journal of Pharmacy and Pharmacology. 2012;**64**:832-842. DOI: 10.1111/j.2042-7158.2012.01492.x

[31] Braga MA, Martini MF, Pickholz M, et al. Clonidine complexation with hydroxypropyl-beta-cyclodextrin: From physico-chemical characterization to in vivo adjuvant effect in local anesthesia. Journal of Pharmaceutical and Biomedical Analysis. 2016;**119**:27-36. DOI: 10.1016/j.jpba.2015.11.015

[32] Korchowiec B, Korchowiec J, Gorczyca M, et al. Molecular organization of nalidixate conjugated calixarenes in bacterial model membranes probed by molecular dynamics simulation and Langmuir monolayer studies. The Journal of Physical Chemistry. B. 2015;**119**:2990-3000. DOI: 10.1021/jp507151r

[33] Paulo PMR, Lopes JNC, Costa SMB. Molecular dynamics simulations of charged dendrimers: Low-to-intermediate half-generation PAMAMs. The Journal of Physical Chemistry. B. 2007;**111**:10651-10664. DOI: 10.1021/jp072211x

[34] Aoun B, Sharma VK, Pellegrini E, et al. Structure and dynamics of ionic micelles: MD simulation and neutron scattering study. The Journal of Physical Chemistry B. 2015;**119**:5079-5086. DOI: 10.1021/acs.jpcb.5b00020

[35] Samanta S, Roccatano D. Interaction of curcumin with PEO–PPO–PEO block copolymers: A molecular dynamics study. The Journal of Physical Chemistry. B. 2013;**117**:3250-3257. DOI: 10.1021/jp309476u

[36] Wood I, Pickholz M. Concentration effects of sumatriptan on the properties of model membranes by molecular dynamics simulations. European Biophysics Journal. 2013;**42**:833-841. DOI: 10.1007/s00249-013-0932-y

[37] Wood I, Pickholz M. Triptan partition in model membranes. Journal of Molecular Modeling. 2014;**20**:1-8. DOI: 10.1007/s00894-014-2463-6

[38] Chew CF, Guy A, Biggin PC. Distribution and dynamics of adamantanes in a lipid bilayer. Biophysical Journal. 2008;**95**:5627-5636. DOI: 10.1529/biophysj.108.139477

[39] Jia Z, O'Mara ML, Zuegg J, et al. The effect of environment on the recognition and binding of vancomycin to native and resistant forms of lipid II. Biophysical Journal. 2011;**101**:2684-2692. DOI: 10.1016/j.bpj.2011.10.047

[40] Cramariuc O, Rog T, Javanainen M, et al. Mechanism for translocation of fluoroquinolones across lipid membranes. Biochimica et Biophysica Acta (BBA)-Biomembranes. 2012;**1818**:2563-2571. DOI: 10.1016/j.bbamem.2012.05.027

[41] Zervou M, Cournia Z, Potamitis C, et al. Insights into the molecular basis of action of the AT1 antagonist losartan using a combined NMR spectroscopy and computational approach. Biochimica et Biophysica Acta (BBA)-Biomembranes. 2014;**1838**:1031-1046. DOI: 10.1016/j.bbamem.2013.12.012

[42] Tu KM, Matubayasi N, Liang KK, et al. A possible molecular mechanism for the pressure reversal of general anaesthetics: Aggregation of halothane in POPC bilayers at high pressure. Chemical Physics Letters. 2012;**543**:148-154. DOI: 10.1016/j.cplett.2012.06.044

[43] Neumann A, Wieczor M, Zielinska J, et al. Membrane sterols modulate the binding mode of amphotericin B without affecting its affinity for a lipid bilayer. Langmuir. 2016;**32**:3452-3461. DOI: 10.1021/acs.langmuir.5b04433

[44] Aliste MP, MacCallum JL, Tieleman DP. Molecular dynamics simulations of pentapeptides at interfaces: Salt bridge and cation-π interactions. Biochemistry. 2003;**42**:8976-8987. DOI: 10.1021/bi027001j

[45] Barlow DJ, Thornton JM. Ion-pairs in proteins. Journal of Molecular Biology. 1983;**168**:867-885

[46] Kumar S, Nussinov R. Salt bridge stability in monomeric proteins. Journal of Molecular Biology. 1999;**293**:1241-1255. DOI: 10.1006/jmbi.1999.3218

[47] Pickholz M, Fernandes Fraceto L, de Paula E. Distribution of neutral prilocaine in a phospholipid bilayer: Insights from molecular dynamics simulations. International Journal of Quantum Chemistry. 2008;**108**:2386-2391. DOI: 10.1002/qua.21767

[48] Högberg C-J, Maliniak A, Lyubartsev AP. Dynamical and structural properties of charged and uncharged lidocaine in a lipid bilayer. Biophysical Chemistry. 2007;**125**:416-424. DOI: 10.1016/j.bpc.2006.10.005

[49] de Paula E, Schreier S, Jarrell HC, Fraceto LF. Preferential location of lidocaine and etidocaine in lecithin bilayers as determined by EPR, fluorescence and 2H NMR. Biophysical Chemistry. 2008;**132**:47-54. DOI: 10.1016/j.bpc.2007.10.004

[50] Pickholz M, Fraceto LF, de Paula E. Preferential location of prilocaine and etidocaine in phospholipid bilayers: A molecular dynamics study. Synthetic Metals. 2009;**159**:2157-2158. DOI: 10.1016/j.synthmet.2009.07.034

[51] Martini MF, Pickholz M. Molecular dynamics study of uncharged bupivacaine enantiomers in phospholipid bilayers. International Journal of Quantum Chemistry. 2012;**112**:3341-3345. DOI: 10.1002/qua.24208

[52] Mojumdar EH, Lyubartsev AP. Molecular dynamics simulations of local anesthetic articaine in a lipid bilayer. Biophysical Chemistry. 2010;**153**:27-35. DOI: 10.1016/j. bpc.2010.10.001

[53] Saeedi M, Lyubartsev AP, Jalili S. Anesthetics mechanism on a DMPC lipid membrane model: Insights from molecular dynamics simulations. Biophysical Chemistry. 2017;**226**:1-13. DOI: 10.1016/j.bpc.2017.03.006

[54] Seelig J. Deuterium magnetic resonance: Theory and application to lipid membranes. Quarterly Reviews of Biophysics. 1977;**10**:353-418

[55] Burnett LJ, Muller BH. Deuteron quadrupole coupling constants in three solid deuterated paraffin hydrocarbons: C2D6, C4D10, C6D14. The Journal of Chemical Physics. 1971;**55**:5829-5831. DOI: 10.1063/1.1675758

[56] Bergamaschi F, Balle VR, Gomes MEW, et al. Levobupivacaína versus bupivacaína em anestesia peridural para cesarianas: Estudo comparativo. Revista Brasileira de Anestesiologia. 2005;**55**(6):606-613. DOI: 10.1590/S0034-70942005000600003

[57] Cabeça LF, Pickholz M, de Paula E, Marsaioli AJ. Liposome-prilocaine interaction mapping evaluated through STD NMR and molecular dynamics simulations. The Journal of Physical Chemistry. B. 2009;**113**:2365-2370. DOI: 10.1021/jp8069496

[58] Butterworth JF, Strichartz GR. Molecular mechanisms of local anesthesia: A review. Anesthesiology. 1990;**72**:711-734

[59] Pickholz M, Giupponi G. Coarse grained simulations of local anesthetics encapsulated into a liposome. The Journal of Physical Chemistry. B. 2010;**114**:7009-7015. DOI: 10.1021/jp909148n

[60] Malheiros SV, Pinto LM, Gottardo L, et al. A new look at the hemolytic effect of local anesthetics, considering their real membrane/water partitioning at pH 7.4. Biophysical Chemistry. 2004;**110**:213-221. DOI: 10.1016/j.bpc.2004.01.013

[61] Karjiban RA, Basri M, Rahman MBA, Salleh AB. Structural properties of nonionic Tween80 micelle in water elucidated by molecular dynamics simulation. APCBEE Procedia. 2012;**3**:287-297. DOI: 10.1016/j.apcbee.2012.06.084

[62] Kuramochi H, Andoh Y, Yoshii N, Okazaki S. All-atom molecular dynamics study of a spherical micelle composed of N-acetylated poly(ethylene glycol) – poly(γ-benzylglutamate) block copolymers: A potential carrier of drug delivery systems for cancer. The Journal of Physical Chemistry. B. 2009;**113**:15181-15188. DOI: 10.1021/jp906155z

[63] Li Y, Hou T. Computational simulation of drug delivery at molecular level. Current Medicinal Chemistry. 2010;**17**:4482-4491. DOI: 21062256

[64] Sutton D, Nasongkla N, Blanco E, Gao J. Functionalized micellar systems for cancer targeted drug delivery. Pharmaceutical Research. 2007;**24**:1029-1046. DOI: 10.1007/s11095-006-9223-y

[65] Xu W, Ling P, Zhang T. Polymeric micelles, a promising drug delivery system to enhance bioavailability of poorly water-soluble drugs. Journal of Drug Delivery. 2013;**2013**:1-15. DOI: 10.1155/2013/340315

[66] Gong J, Chen M, Zheng Y, et al. Polymeric micelles drug delivery system in oncology. Journal of Controlled Release. 2012;**159**:312-323. DOI: 10.1016/j.jconrel.2011.12.012

[67] Schmidt RK, Teo B, Brady JW. Use of umbrella sampling in the calculation of the potential of mean force for maltose in vacuum from molecular dynamics simulations. The Journal of Physical Chemistry. 1995;**99**:11339-11343. DOI: 10.1021/j100029a007

[68] Babin V, Karpusenka V, Moradi M, et al. Adaptively biased molecular dynamics: An umbrella sampling method with a time-dependent potential. International Journal of Quantum Chemistry. 2009;**109**:3666-3678. DOI: 10.1002/qua.22413

[69] Comer J, Gumbart JC, Hénin J, et al. The adaptive biasing force method: Everything you always wanted to know but were afraid to ask. The Journal of Physical Chemistry. B. 2015;**119**:1129-1151. DOI: 10.1021/jp506633n

[70] Nagasima T, Kinjo AR, Mitsui T, Nishikawa K. Wang-Landau molecular dynamics technique to search for low-energy conformational space of proteins. Physical Review E. 2007;**75**:66706. DOI: 10.1103/PhysRevE.75.066706

[71] Patel JS, Berteotti A, Ronsisvalle S, et al. Steered molecular dynamics simulations for studying protein–ligand interaction in cyclin-dependent kinase 5. Journal of Chemical Information and Modeling. 2014;**54**:470-480. DOI: 10.1021/ci4003574

[72] Loverde SM, Klein ML, Discher DE. Nanoparticle shape improves delivery: Rational coarse grain molecular dynamics (rCG-MD) of taxol in worm-like PEG-PCL micelles. Advanced Materials. 2012;**24**:3823-3830. DOI: 10.1002/adma.201103192

[73] Swails JM, York DM, Roitberg AE. Constant pH replica exchange molecular dynamics in explicit solvent using discrete protonation states: Implementation, testing, and validation. Journal of Chemical Theory and Computation. 2014;**10**:1341-1352. DOI: 10.1021/ct401042b

[74] Simonsen JB. Evaluation of reconstituted high-density lipoprotein (rHDL) as a drug delivery platform — A detailed survey of rHDL particles ranging from biophysical properties to clinical implications. Nanomedicine: Nanotechnology, Biology and Medicine. 2016;**12**:2161-2179. DOI: 10.1016/j.nano.2016.05.009

[75] Meneksedag-Erol D, Tang T, Uludağ H. Mechanistic insights into the role of glycosaminoglycans in delivery of polymeric nucleic acid nanoparticles by molecular dynamics simulations. Biomaterials. 2018;**156**:107-120. DOI: 10.1016/j.biomaterials.2017.11.037

www.ingramcontent.com/pod-product-compliance
Lightning Source LLC
Chambersburg PA
CBHW081232190326
41458CB00016B/5754